THE MYSTERY OF JESUS
OF JESUS FROM
GENESIS TO REVELATION
YESTERDAY, TODAY, AND TOMORROW

THE
MYSTERY
OF JESUS FROM
GENESIS TO REVELATION

YESTERDAY, TODAY, AND TOMORROW

—— VOLUME THREE ——
THE APOCALYPSE

Dr. Thomas R. Horn, Donna Howell, Allie Anderson

DEFENDER

CRANE

The Mystery of Jesus from Genesis to Revelation: Yesterday, Today, and Tomorrow
Volume Three: The Apocalypse
By Dr. Thomas R. Horn, Donna Howell, Allie Anderson

All Scripture is taken from the King James Version of the Bible unless otherwise noted.

Cover design by Jeffrey Mardis

ISBN: 978-1-948014-63-2

CONTENTS

VOLUME THREE

THE APOCALYPSE

Not counting far-sighted prophecies in Daniel, Isaiah, and other Old and New Testament visions of the future, up to this point, each of the sixty-five other books of the Bible were in and of the *past*. Revelation—also called "Apocalypse" and "Apocalypse of John"—though written in the past, is a prophecy about the *future*. In other words, the book is based on "revelations" or visions given by Christ, Himself, to John, of events that have not yet taken place. (Thus the name. Despite common use of "Revelations," plural, the proper name for this book is singular.) When these events do occur, they will bring a momentous and final conclusion to all that God has purposed for the human race from the beginning of Creation forward.

When the tragic terrorist attack on the Twin Towers occurred on September 11, 2001 (9/11), near the start of this century, many Americans suddenly got a *lot* more interested in what this "old book" had to say. Polls taken in 2002 showed that more than one-third of Americans experienced a sharp increase in their interest in the Bible as a result of the attack; though only 39 percent of those polled believed the Bible to be the written Word of God, a staggering 59 percent stated that John's enigmatic vision was coming true in their day. In fact, nearly one-fifth agreed they would live to see the end of the world, while one-fourth believed 9/11 could be interpreted as having been predicted in Revelation, proving that "many other Americans who usually ignore the Bible are willing to listen to teachers of Bible prophecy when world events reach crisis levels."[1] We can imagine that, when we do get closer to the end times, events such as 9/11 will increase in number and intensity due to spiritual warfare if nothing else. When those days come, we may just be looking at a revival or a Great Awakening of the saints on the ground prior to that glorious day when we are taken up to be with Christ in the air. That will be one last upsurge in the number of God's people on earth before a final, pre-Rapture harvest.

That is, however, just *one* way to interpret the text...

SETTING OF REVELATION

Let us first briefly discuss the book of Revelation's setting. From there, we will address its various interpretations, then examine its content.

Authorship, Canonicity, and Setting

In our look at the previous sixty-five books of the Bible, we haven't spent much time or space on parsing out the details of authorship and canonicity. However, for reasons we are about to discuss, the setting of the book's writing—Patmos—somewhat calls for at least a brief reflection. We, along with most scholars, believe Revelation, sometimes referred to as "Apocalypse," was written by Apostle John, the same author who produced the fourth Gospel, as well as the Epistles of 1, 2, and 3 John. As we read from Eusebius' *Ecclesiastical History* (who also quotes from Irenaeus), John was deported to the island of Patmos during the time of Emperor Domitian:

It is said that in this persecution the apostle and evangelist John, who was still alive, was condemned to dwell on the island of Patmos in consequence of his testimony to the divine word.

Irenaeus, in the fifth book of his work *Against Heresies*, where he discusses the number of the name of Antichrist which is given in the so-called Apocalypse of John, speaks as follows concerning him:

"If it were necessary for his name to be proclaimed openly at the present time, it would have been declared by him who saw the revelation. For it was seen not long ago, but almost in our own generation, at the end of the reign of Domitian."

To such a degree, indeed, did the teaching of our faith flourish at that time that even those writers who were far from our religion did not hesitate to mention in their histories the persecution and the martyrdoms which took place during it.[2]

Despite Eusebius' massive sway in the topic of early Church history—and his outright attribution of the writing of "Apocalypse" to the "Apostle John" and "the apostle and evangelist John" in what we just read—conclusions about Revelation's authorship did not go unchallenged in former times. Some believe the Revelator was a prophet in the early Church who had travelled around Asia Minor, thus giving him unique familiarity with the seven churches mentioned in the book. During the second century, Justin Martyr (in his *Dialogue with Trypho*; 81.4) and Bishop Irenaeus (in his *Against Heresies*; 4.20.11) both agreed with our conclusion (and Eusebius') that John the Revelator was the apostle, son of Zebedee. Irenaeus' testimony is one that should be heeded, as he was a disciple of the teachings of Polycarp, who personally knew John the apostle and attributed Revelation to his writing.

A Roman Church elder by the name of Gaius around the same time said the book was written by Cerinthus, a troublemaker in the Church. Another man, Bishop Dionysius of Alexandria (according to

Eusebius; *Ecclesiastical History* 7.25), believed the book too enigmatic to match the writing style of the Apostle John and claimed it had simply been written by another man with the same common name. The apostle's "diction of the Gospel and Epistle differs from that of the Apocalypse,"[3] Dionysius says. He goes on to say that:

> ...the writer had...the gift of knowledge and the gift of expression,—as the Lord had bestowed them both upon him.... I perceive, however, that his dialect and language...uses barbarous idioms....
>
> I would not have any one think that I have said these things in a spirit of ridicule, for I have said what I have only with the purpose of showing clearly the difference between the writings.[4]

In his lengthier discussion, Dionysius also points out that the Revelator oddly taught "that the kingdom of Christ will be an earthly one,"[5] which is one of the reasons questions were raised about the book's qualification for inclusion within the canon. Jesus taught that His Kingdom was "not of this world," which initially appeared to contradict the teachings of the early Church (and understandably so) that the book of Revelation describes Christ's Millennial Reign *on earth*. But there is a chief reason this should not be a worry for us (and one of the reasons this particular argument was eventually dropped in the debate of the book's canonicity). While Jesus was teaching about His Kingdom, He was a resident of our current world, which, in its sinful state, belongs to Satan (2 Corinthians 4:4; Ephesians 2:2; John 12:31). All of this changes in Revelation 11:15, when "the kingdoms of this world are become the kingdoms of our Lord, and of his Christ." Therefore, it's correct to say that Christ's Kingdom would not be considered a threat to the politicians of His day (though they didn't understand this), but in nearing the end of Revelation—*after* the kingdoms of this world have been placed under the power of Christ—He will reign in "this world" *and* in the unseen realm.

By no means was this the only wrinkle that had to be ironed out prior to the Spirit-guided decision to include it in the canon. We don't have the time or space to dedicate the next fifty pages to every issue raised in that debate, but with one example, we can show that the same interpretational issues that plague us today regarding Revelation were present from the beginning. In fact, though Dionysius himself agreed that the book was canonical, his early sentiments about its mystery often mirror those of our own. He states:

> But I suppose that it is beyond my comprehension, and that there is a certain concealed and more wonderful meaning in every part. For if I do not understand I suspect that a deeper sense lies beneath the words.
>
> I do not measure and judge them by my own reason, but leaving the more to faith I regard them as too high for me to grasp. And I do not reject what I cannot comprehend, but rather wonder because I do not understand it.[6]

If we're honest, many Christians today—even those in the most highly respected offices in the world of academia—acknowledge that we feel the same way this early bishop did when we read the Revelation. We don't dispute its authority, but we frequently say, "It's above my head," or, "I generally understand its apocalyptic nature, but I don't grasp its symbolism."

Coming round about: In an ironic (and perhaps backward) way, this intense confusion serves as one of the grandest arguments in favor of John the Evangelist (apostle and son of Zebedee) as the author. From the beginning, interpreting Revelation has been so difficult that, had it been written by anyone *other* than an apostle of Christ, the question about its canonicity would have been magnified. For who would agree to place within the Holy Word a book that almost nobody can easily understand and whose author was "just some nice guy from the first century" who had accumulated some followers by telling them of his bizarre dreams and visions? As we've seen from almost every Epistle in the New Testament, anyone claiming God had given them a vision that didn't align with the teachings of the apostles were called "false teachers" and "false prophets." Though Revelation *does agree* with the apostolic voices of the first century (in fact, it authenticates all of Scripture, from Genesis forward), interpretational problems like the "not of this world" issue we just addressed initially suggest that it might not. Such a controversial document would have been disregarded immediately and tossed into the huge pile of extrabiblical, apocryphal books had it not been widely received as a teaching from a true apostle who tied it into the prophetic messages of both the Old and New Testaments.

If the writing were *not* from of the son of Zebedee, the Revelator would have to be: 1) well-known by all the early churches that contributed to the book's circulation; 2) authoritative enough to expect these churches to take his warnings seriously; 3) so strong and intimidating in his teaching that the government at the time would see him as a threat, making him fit for exile to Patmos; 4) well-versed in the Old Testament prophecies that are frequently referenced in the book; 5) well-versed in Koine Greek; 6) willing to use theological concepts that are unique to those of the Apostle John's Gospel, such as Jesus being viewed as "the Word" (and many others); 7) able to explain why Polycarp, who personally knew the son of Zebedee, was wrong when he confidently taught others (including Irenaeus) that the Evangelist and the Revelator were one and the same;[7] and 8) an authoritative apostle of the same time whose name also happened to be "John." The likelihood that there was another "John" at the time with the apostle's influence and who satisfies the qualifications on this list—and of whom we, today, don't know anything about from the huge collection of historical documents detailing the writers of the Word—causes overwhelming doubt.

We will therefore proceed with the firm conclusion that the author of Revelation is the same as that of the Gospel of John, and 1, 2, and

3 John: It is the Apostle John, son of Zebedee, the Evangelist, and the Elder, who is now also known by the moniker "the Revelator." However, note that in this book, John is called a "prophet" as well (Revelation 22:9).

The Island of Patmos

The small, volcanic island of Patmos is in the Icarian Sea (a subdivision of the Aegean Sea), just southwest from the coastline of Asia Minor (a little over thirty-five miles southwest from Miletus). It is one of twelve Greco-Roman islands collectively called "the Dodecanese." The distinct shape of the land mass makes it look like a seahorse swimming to the right.

Many of us, when we read that John was exiled to an island, imagine a scenario resembling the circumstances of Tom Hank's character, Chuck Noland, in the popular film *Cast Away*. We wonder if, perhaps, John had a similar experience, huddling under exotic plants during harsh weather; eating worms and bugs; building fires by rubbing sticks together; shivering in dark caves; watching the coastlines for rescue ships; and making a "friend" out of a log or coconut to give him company and to talk to between writing sessions—in the same manner Noland famously designed his best friend "Wilson" from a volleyball manufactured by Wilson Sporting Goods.

Such a setting could certainly contribute to a heavy loneliness that could lead to hysterical thoughts—maybe even hallucinations—that would affect the integrity of the book. If John was entirely cut off from the human race and existed as one man on an island surrounded by water as far as the eye could see, surely his imagination would have run wild, leading to bizarre, or even apocalyptic, ideas. How, then, could we trust what he saw in the visions he described in Revelation? (Biblical artwork sometimes contributes to this concept by depicting imagery of an old, bearded John sitting on sharp rocks next to withered trees—alone, and looking out into the endless sea with no belongings other than a quill and parchment.)

However, in spite of the logic behind our ideas about John and his surroundings, a look at the geographical history of Patmos reveals our concepts are based on a grave misunderstanding perpetuated by human imagination and art; they're not at all based on reality.

First of all, if Eusebius' account of history is correct, then John was only exiled to Patmos for about a year and a half. That's not nearly as dramatic as what happened to Hanks' emaciated character, who lived entirely alone for four years. That brings us to our second point: The Romans of John's day frequently used such islands as Patmos to exile people who threatened them, and Patmos had already established some level of civilization as early as the Middle Bronze Age or the Mycenaean Era of Greece (circa 1700–1100 BC), as extant pottery in and around the area dates. The island featured a well-developed seaport at a location known in New Testament times as Phora (today, "Skala"), situated on the eastern side between the "neck" and the "abdomen" of the island's seahorse shape. Likewise, after stating that Patmos was one of several islands the Milesians (residents of Miletus) inhabited for military purposes from the late seventh century BC through John's day, the *Lexham Geographic Commentary on Acts through Revelation* further explains:

> Patmos formed part of a second line of islands comprising Miletus' commercial sphere.... Patmos also played a critical defensive role in protecting Miletus' commercial routes. With Leros and Lepsi, Patmos was a *phrourion* (..."military fortress"). Milesian veterans formed an important population within the colony. The island was governed by a phrourarch (...*phrourarchos*) [a] commanding officer of the garrison. The island's social, political, and economic life was thus oriented to Miletus for centuries.[8]

When John was exiled, he would have been dropped off at a populated seaport (possibly Phora), where he would have immediately come face to face with commercial activity under the supervision of the Milesian government. From there, he *may* have decided to travel south to a cave that later traditions marked as the site of John's visions (just below the contemporary location of the monastery of St. John the Divine), but he would have easily been within walking distance to civilization. Scholars have good reason (drawn from historical accounts) to believe that, a year and a half later, John returned to Ephesus during the reign of Nerva, resuming his post as pastor of Ephesus.[9] Most other legends of John's time on the island come from the *Acts of John*, which is not a reliable source, as it was claimed to have been written by John's scribe, but it was dated to the fifth century AD (hundreds of years after John or anyone claiming to be his scribe could have lived). It is thus a work that falls into a category of literature known as the Pseudepigrapha (texts written by people under pseudonyms—falsely attributed works) and cannot be trusted to contain truth (unlike apocryphal works, which generally have more solid attribution).

Audience and Occasion

With Revelation's authorship, canonicity, and setting established, the occasion for the letter is unique from any other in the Word, as John experienced prophetic and futuristic visions that had not yet come true (as stated prior), and he wished to circulate the information to the early Church as a warning. More specifically, the text was delivered to an audience of seven churches of his day (Ephesus, Smyrna, Pergamum, Thyatira, Sardis, Philadelphia, and Laodicea—each addressed in the coming pages), while on a wider scale, we can safely assume from Revelation 1:3 (an exhortation and blessing meant for *all* in the Church who read it) that John believed the Holy Spirit intended everyone in the Church of all times to have a copy and heed it. What a blessing for us, today, that circulation attempt was successful when he returned to Ephesus, as we have the book in our canon now. Our next issue, then, is why we keep saying the book covers matters that are *yet to come*, as some disagree.

Varying Approaches to Interpretation

As is inherent in apocalyptic literature, symbolism is rich throughout. This naturally places a lot of responsibility on the reader, whose own imagination as to what these texts are saying can, unfortunately, come up with endless speculation. One immense help in deciphering Revelation is consulting the rest of the Old and New Testaments, which helps "qualify" what is being described whenever the human mind fails: When we read of something bizarre occurring, we can search Scripture to see if anything similar is mentioned elsewhere. Despite this major tool, there are still questions about whether the symbols and signs of Revelation point to literal or figurative fulfillment, as well as to past, present, or future fulfillment.

Modern scholars adhere to some of the following approaches far more than others. Though the authors of this book maintain a futurist outlook, we do not disrespect those who interpret it differently. Many ideas floating around in the academic world say that there are about six to eight different interpretational methods regarding the Revelation, but scholars agree that most folks land in one of the following four categories. (Note that these summaries are intentionally oversimplified. Our purpose is to look at them generally. One might find exceptions to our generalizations, and we anticipate that. A far more in-depth view regarding how each of these differs from the next and a more complete list of arguments for or against any of these interpretational methods can be found in hundreds of alternate sources. To keep this book clean of irrelevant information, we'll address these subjects briefly.)

Idealist: This approach also falls under the labels "nonhistorical," "spiritual," or "poetic," and it states that the whole work of Revelation is allegory, determining righteous principles to live by at all times. This view sees the struggle between good and evil in general, portraying God as victorious throughout all time. Naturally, there is no true "event(s)" the text can be tied to in such a method.

Our problem with this view: For this method to hold, we must disregard details in Revelation that are precise and specific, such as time markers (for example, Revelation 11:2, mentioning forty-two months). Likewise, the "fulfillment" of key, end-time religious and political figures are much harder to explain in this view, and when they are, the explanations seem insufficient. Most importantly: If no "event" can be tied to Revelation, then a *lot* of prophecy found in the rest of the Bible (both Testaments) is voided.

Preterist: Also referred to as the "contemporary-historical" method, this is the view that Revelation's prophesied events have already taken place in the past; more specifically, the imagery relates to what was going on between Christians and Rome in John's day. Persecution of the early Church, the fall of Rome, and the destruction of the Temple would all be examples of this.

Our problem with this view: Revelation is distinctly and repeatedly called a prophecy (1:3; 22:7, 10, 18–19). Prophecy, *in the context of apocalyptic literature*, looks forward to things that could not have happened at the time the literature was penned. (Note that if the most widely accepted dating of the early centuries is accurate, Revelation was written in AD 95, during the reign of Emperor Domitian, well after such occurrences as the fall of Rome or destruction of the Temple. So how could a prophecy of the future in AD 95 "look forward" to something that happened about twenty-five years before its writing?) This view also calls for us to disregard specifics. For example, Revelation 9:18 says one-third of mankind would be killed, and this did not happen at any point during or around John's day (or between his day and now, further supporting that this is yet to come).

Historicist: Alternatively called the "Church history" or "Church-historical" view (or other similar, equivalent terms), this is the idea that the focus of Revelation is entirely about the history of the Church from the date of its writing to the time of Christ's return (the entire "Church Age"). Adherents of this view are not, like the preterists, limited to the scope of events occurring in John's day, but to any event the individual interpreter believes to have been a fulfillment at any point, including very recent history (ongoing until the Second Advent).

Our problem with this view: It opens a can of worms wherein anyone can see the fulfillment of prophecy each time they watch the news. No two interpreters appear to agree on what is represented by Revelation's symbolism, which is an interpretational nightmare. For instance, the angel or star named "Wormwood" that falls to earth (see Revelation 8:10–11), causing one-third of the earth's water to become poisonous, is viewed by some to have been fulfilled in the Chernobyl nuclear disaster in the Ukraine in 1986: the radioactive fallout is the "black herb" (*chernobyl,* linked by some to the herb also known as wormwood) that made the environment around the nuclear plant uninhabitable. We don't believe this connection responsibly fulfills the prophecy regarding one-third of all the world's clean water in a city that, before the reactor incident, maxed out at a population of only fourteen thousand people and, after the tragedy, caused a derelict "exclusion zone" of only approximately twenty square miles. (Note that the contamination area is larger than this. But even while taking into consideration the farthest extent of the affected zone in areas that are technically still inhabitable, with clean water, a generous estimate doesn't allow for more than a hundred square miles around the reactor, or three hundred square miles if you travel directly north of the site where most pollution was carried after the explosion. The earth's water—just water, by itself—calculates to barely under 140 *million* square miles, so "one-third" of the water being poisoned as a result of Chernobyl is not even close to a fair comparison.) Nor do we, after an exhaustive dip into the etymology of the word "wormwood," find any true link between the herb with the same name and the star/angel that falls from the sky. (This etymological trail is irrelevant here, but for those who are interested in our conclusions regarding these terms, Thomas Horn's book, *The Wormwood Prophecy*, debunks common assumptions about these verses and the history of language associated with wormwood, including references to it in the Old Testament.) Additionally, the historicist view forces Revelation to be isolated from other books of the Bible that describe the same events in similar, but clearly unfulfilled, ways (such as 2 Thessalonians 2:3, which tells that Jesus' return will follow the rising up of the Antichrist, who causes the worldwide "falling away" from the Church as well as *many* passages from the Old Testament describing the Millennial Reign).

Futurist: A "literal" interpretation…though by "literal," we don't mean that Satan is a red dragon with ten horns and seven heads and so on, but that the symbolic language of Revelation foresees actual events of the future with real people: A "king" could represent a literal president or politician with extreme executive power over earthly "king-doms" (countries, states, etc.), even though exact words like "kings" and "kingdoms" may be rendered obsolete by the time of Revelation's fulfillment. Since this book might be reaching folks who are unfamil-iar with Revelation, let's state this another way: The new believers of Christ's time saw the fulfillment of the Old Testament references to "the Branch" in Jesus. Obviously, Jesus was a real human Messiah (not discounting His role as also deity), and not part of a plant that grows out from the trunk of a tree like branches do. But prophecies about this Branch were also *not* about some invisible or metaphorical ele-ment that fits into the grand scheme of good versus evil, either. Just as the "Branch" was a real Person—a literal fulfillment of prophetic, figu-rative "Branch" language—the characters and events of Revelation will be literal fulfillments of prophetic, figurative language (dragons, beasts, etc.). In this view, most of the frightening events from Revelation will escalate at the end of all time, right before the Second Advent of the Messiah, and the fortunate events for believers will follow.

We do not find a problem in this view, and we are, ourselves, futurists.

Despite the name of this interpretational method, even the most dedicated futurists acknowledge that some of the events did occur in the past (almost all agree that this includes Revelation chapters 1–3 involving the letters to the churches of Asia Minor at that time) while we await the fulfillment of others. (You will see how this shift from past events to future ones naturally occurs in the narrative of John's visions when we get there.) Some of these concepts are often broken down into groups that fit into an "already-happened" versus a "hasn't-happened-yet" label, and sometimes it's both: Christ's warnings "already happened" with the churches the letters were written to, while they still apply to us today, and therefore have "not yet happened" in our time. Although this sounds complicated, one quick and easy way to illustrate these concepts is to look at our own current salvation status.

The Word says that when we accept Christ, we become "a new creature: old things are passed away; behold, all things are become new" (2 Corinthians 5:17). That is, while we are in this world and in our current physical state, we "already" become something we weren't before, and the proof of that is observable in a changed nature. The Holy Spirit—if believers are sincere—is invited in and allowed to convict. Our old habits are passed away, and a relationship with God replaces any relationships we've had with pornography, alcohol, drugs, casual hook-ups at the bar, or whatever our individual's vices might have been. Even smaller things, like giving someone "the bird" for cutting us off in traffic or being grumbly in a long line at the grocery store, are slowly uprooted and traded for righteous behavior. Or, perhaps the change is an internal one: We have faith in God where there was hopelessness before, or joy that overwhelms our sorrow. However it manifests, an authentic conversion from one who is lost into one who belongs to the Family of God can, and does, make that person new. This is the realization of salvation *here*, while we live on the earth. But because we give our lives to Jesus while we live in these bodies—the "already"—we will experience another change *there*, on the other side of this life, passing into eternity with perfect bodies like Christ's post-Resurrection body, and perfected spiritual status, dwelling in the presence of God for all eternity: this is the full consummation of a biblical promise that completes the "not yet" side of our blessed hope. The "already" and "not yet" theology is apparent in some places of the book of Revelation. (We mostly explained all this to help readers who hear teachings about this by others in church or other venues of biblical study. Our book's goal is to avoid confusing terminology wherever possible, so we won't go into much of the already/not yet discussion. But since so many today are turning to more impersonal presentations of the Word—such as YouTube sermons, studies on ministry websites, etc.—we want to explain this for your benefit because it's not easy to approach these "distant" teachers personally with questions.)

Also, early on in the study of biblical prophecy, it's important to know about a concept called "dual [or "double"] fulfillment": the idea that a prophecy in the Bible can refer to more than one fulfillment. (This is sometimes referred to as "short-term" vs. "long-term" fulfillments.) Historically, this concept has introduced some controversy. For example, Theodore of Mopsuestia, a Christian theologian from the earlier centuries (circa 350–428), would not believe that a single prophecy could refer to more than one future event. From his time forward, a number of well-trained theologians and scholars have agreed with him, and their concerns are valid: If we acknowledge the possibility of dual fulfillment, what stops us from opening another can of worms by saying that every headline on the news is the actualization of something foreseen? Eventually, that approach would make Christianity somewhat of a joke to unbelievers who observe from the outside that none of us agree or, more pejoratively stated, "Christians don't even know *what* they believe." (Consider how many possible "marks of the Beast" [the Antichrist] that have been brought to attention through the years. For example, most recently, Christian social media has been ablaze with warnings that the COVID-19 vaccine is "*the* mark." One of Howell's friends called her in a panic a couple of months ago asking her about this, and by the end of the conversation, this friend was comforted to learn that we still had time, as Howell explained various other prophecies from Revelation that have not yet been fulfilled, and the vaccine could not therefore be Antichrist's prophesied, mandatory mark. Confusion like this is simply a part of what happens when the human race is given a peek into the supreme plan of a deity whose ways and thoughts are not *our* ways and thoughts [Isaiah 55:8–9]. Other "marks" have been improperly identified as being anything from credit cards to medical-history chips. We will discuss the mark later on, but suffice it to say here that it will be introduced alongside a mandatory-worship plan by a major political leader when it does occur, so that is one thing to watch for.)

On the other hand, the Bible itself tends to favor the likelihood of dual fulfillment. For example: We frequently see Joel's prophecy in chapters 2 and 3 about the Holy Spirit as referring to the Day of Pentecost. In order to illustrate the duality, we need to look at the *whole* prophecy:

> And it shall come to pass afterward, that I will pour out my spirit upon all flesh; and your sons and your daughters shall prophesy, your old men shall dream dreams, your young men shall see visions: And also upon the servants and upon the handmaids in those days will I pour out my spirit. And I will shew wonders in the heavens and in the earth, blood, and fire, and pillars of smoke. The sun shall be turned into darkness, and the moon into blood, before the great and terrible day of the Lord come. And it shall come to pass, that whosoever shall call on the name of the Lord shall be delivered: for in mount Zion and in Jerusalem shall be deliverance, as the Lord hath said, and in the remnant whom the Lord shall call. For, behold, in those days, and in that time, when I shall bring again the captivity of Judah and Jerusalem, I will also gather all nations,

and will bring them down into the valley of Jehoshaphat, and will plead with them there for my people and for my heritage Israel, whom they have scattered among the nations, and parted my land. (Joel 2:28–3:2)

In Acts, we read of a fulfillment of this prophecy, as acknowledged by Peter, himself, before a crowd of witnesses:

But Peter, standing up with the eleven, lifted up his voice, and said unto them, "Ye men of Judaea, and all ye that dwell at Jerusalem, be this known unto you, and hearken to my words…this is that which was spoken by the prophet Joel; 'And it shall come to pass in the last days, saith God, I will pour out of my Spirit upon all flesh: and your sons and your daughters shall prophesy, and your young men shall see visions, and your old men shall dream dreams: And on my servants and on my handmaidens I will pour out in those days of my Spirit; and they shall prophesy: And I will shew wonders in heaven above, and signs in the earth beneath; blood, and fire, and vapour of smoke: The sun shall be turned into darkness, and the moon into blood, before the great and notable day of the Lord come: And it shall come to pass, that whosoever shall call on the name of the Lord shall be saved.' [Note that this is the end of what Peter quotes from Joel; he then goes on to speak for himself once again:] Ye men of Israel, hear these words; Jesus of Nazareth, a man approved of God among you by miracles and wonders and signs." (Acts 2:14–22)

Both books, Joel and Acts, are canonized as the authoritative written Word of God. We therefore cannot say, "Well, Peter got it wrong. What happened on the Day of Pentecost had nothing to do with what Joel said," unless we are among the minority that dabbles in the dangerous craft of picking and choosing which parts of the Word we will believe and which parts we won't. Therefore, we have no choice but to see that what Joel prophesied *was* fulfilled on the Day of Pentecost. However, Peter gets to a certain point and stops quoting from the prophecy of Joel, even though Joel went on to describe things that *did not* happen on the Day of Pentecost: the gathering of all nations into the Valley of Jehoshaphat, for example. Thus, Joel's prophecy has been "already" fulfilled, while "not yet" at the same time, because we are awaiting the moment when all nations are gathered in this valley and the judgment of God falls upon all people. This event, futurists believe, occurs in the book of Revelation (more on this later). When it does occur in the future, we will have the second part of the "dual [or "double"] fulfillment."

Balance is needed here: Interpreting a single Scripture or passage apart from the rest of the Word's treatment of a topic leads to error. Responsible Christians will not find repetitive fulfillments each time another world event takes place, but, in credit to those who tend to do just this, they *are* watching the signs of the times, and it is these folks who will likely be the first to recognize when prophecies are coming into light in the future. So whereas we cannot applaud every panic, we do commend those who are being open-minded, end-times watchmen of signs.

Not surprisingly, scholars frequently disagree about what events have and have not yet occurred and how they align with Revelation's symbolism, breaking the futurist category into several subcategories, primarily differing in the interpretation of the timing of Christ's thousand-year Millennial Reign on earth (Revelation 20):

Amillennialists: The "a" at the front of the word "amillennialism" here suggests "no millennial." This is an unfortunate title, as amillennialists do believe in *a* Millennial Reign of Christ, but rather, they think it to be metaphorical: They believe Christ is reigning *now*, in this Church Age; no reign of Christ in a visible and earthly manner will occur. Mention of the "one thousand years" is also a metaphor, or a spiritual timeline: The "Millennial Reign" of our Lord began at His

First Coming and ends at His Second Coming. Saints are experiencing this time currently, because we are free to preach the Gospel as the enemy was defeated through the work of the cross.

Our problem with this view: These interpretations offer little hope to Christians today in countries where we are *not* celebrating the reign of Christ, but where we are instead still being persecuted (sometimes to the point of death) for following Him. Therefore, amillennialism is primarily a Western theology that doesn't truly apply worldwide. If we are to believe that this moment in time is the great and wonderful reign of Christ over all the earth, some of this grand promise from Scripture appears bleak in its fulfillment. Also, certain issues arise in this viewpoint that force inconsistent interpretation. For example: The two references to resurrection mentioned in Revelation 20:4–5 are described with identical words, and John's writing doesn't indicate in any way that he is referring to two *different* kinds of resurrection. However, amillennialism, with its emphasis on spiritualizing these events regarding the saints, often asserts the first resurrection to be a spiritual one and the second to be physical. Also, anytime a literal Millennial Reign is diminished to allegory, many, *many* of the Old Testament prophets' words appear to be wrong (see Isaiah 9:6–7; 11:1–5; 40:9–10; Jeremiah 23:5–8; Daniel 7:13–14; Malachi 3:1–2 for just a few examples). And finally, we must ask: If the prophecies of Jesus were fulfilled literally in His First Advent, why wouldn't there be a literal fulfillment of the Millennial Reign involving the same Messiah in His Second Advent?

Postmillennialists: Folks with this perspective believe Christ will return *after* the Millennium, which is a kind of Golden Age wherein Christians will enjoy worldwide influence and prosperity. John's reference to a thousand-year reign is not literal; it simply means "a really long time." Believers therefore are responsible for "Christianizing" the world—realizing the Kingdom of God here, as things get better and better over time—until Jesus sees that this place is worthy of His return, and only then will He come back.

Our problem with this view: To begin with, Revelation clearly and explicitly describes how things will get worse and worse (not better) before Jesus' return. Several verses in the Epistles (for instance, 2 Timothy 3:1–7) also point to the increase of terrible times in these last days. Further, Jesus' Kingdom was "not of this earth," and it won't be until this earth is taken from the enemy and given over to Christ (Revelation 11:15). If a postmillennialist sees Christ's Kingdom as the "Christianizing" of this old world we're currently living in, then we must revisit whether Jesus really meant what He said when He told His captors quite frankly that this current world was *not* His Kingdom. Additionally, we have a hard time believing that Christ, in all His authority, majesty, and power, is waiting on fallen, imperfect humanity—who has, since the time of Adam, messed up repeatedly—to perfect the world and the people within it. Many other hiccups arise in the postmillennialists' allegorical interpretations that cause the meaning of the words in Revelation to become subjective to the reader, and when word definitions are dropped, we arrive, yet again, at the point wherein anyone can claim he or she has the answers to what John says in Revelation. It's a battle, over and over, to get any two Christians to agree on what is really being stated.

(Note, too, that many take "Christianizing the world" to mean an aggressive political stance in favor of a theocratic government. We do believe Christians should vote and be involved in the legislation of their land, but we don't believe that ushering in a president or powerful political group representing God's ideal is the same as a Millennial Reign; such an approach to Scripture would eventually come to embrace Antichrist, who will outwardly uphold God's ideal for his own deceptive purposes in the beginning, ironically fulfilling the opposite of what God wants for His people and bringing in the Beast. However, we have reason to be grateful for postmillennialism. This method became a dominant movement in the eighteenth and nineteenth centuries when Great Awakenings spread across American soil, and the spiritual results were so massively positive for the quickly growing Church that believers thought Christianizing the world was quite possible. Before the Great Awakenings, earlier settlers in the United States were largely amillennial. Yet, once the fever of duty hit these men and women with the promise that their earthly actions toward aggressive evangelizing would usher in the Second Coming, they raised churches, schools, missionary organizations, and all forms of ministry as a bedrock of American life. Essentially, the postmillennial, Puritan activists were the driving force behind how much of the Western world established its God-fearing roots in society. All this goes to show that even when Christian men and women are not united in perfect interpretational harmony, God blesses the sincerity of their hearts toward a reformed religious and social atmosphere on earth. This argues in favor of why interpretational differences regarding Revelation should *never* cause strife or division in the Body as it currently does. Christians can "part ways" on their beliefs about the future, but they must always remain "forever united" in evangelism!)

Premillennialists: Adherents to this thinking believe Christ's return is set to occur *before* the Millennium. The era of peace, or the "Golden Age," is the same era as the Millennium, ushered in by Christ, personally. The Millennial Reign is a literal, visible time in the future when Christ's Kingdom on earth is realized. Put simply: The victory that was accomplished on the cross will be made known to the world and God's enemies when Christ returns. The events of Revelation occur in a specific, chronological order once the visions are aligned, and characters (such as Antichrist) are real people who fulfill true religious and political roles within this order. The climax of the book of Revelation will play out in actual world events leading up to the apocalypse or the destruction of our current planet, which will then be replaced by a New Earth that somewhat resembles the perfection God intended at Creation before the Fall of man. From the correct standpoint that Scripture interprets Scripture (the principle that more than one passage in the whole of the Word helps bring into focus a particular verse), the premillennialist is less likely than some interpreters to read the Bible subjectively and believe any current event on earth is related to something Revelation says, because we take the *whole* of the Word into account in interpreting this one book. We believe the "literal" approach to the Bible is the correct way, unless such an approach creates an absurdity that language, grammar, syntax, and context show to symbolize or illustrate another concept. The premillennialist also allows for 2 Peter 1:20–21 to guide us when it states that no prophecy ever originated from within a prophet or came about by his own interpretations. Some in these previous categories self-interpret, looking for a deeper or more spiritual meaning than the events Revelation otherwise clearly teaches. Finally, in immense support of premillennialism are the words of Christ, Himself, when He said that the Son of Man will come from the heavens "immediately after the tribulation [and among some other astronomical signs]" (Matthew 24:21, 29–30; 25:31). This positions Christ's return—not to be confused with the Rapture of the Church earlier on (in pre-Trib theology, which we will discuss in a moment)—*after* the Tribulation but *before* the Millennial Reign.

Again, we have no problem with this view. We are premillennialists, ourselves.

But it should be stated that even some of our closest associates in ministry fall under some of the former categories of interpreters, and we can (and do) break bread with these fellow believers without allowing our differences to stifle the unity we are commanded in the Word to share. Our biggest issue is not with folks who study the Word and come to a conclusion that's different from ours, but with folks who come to a rigid conclusion without truly studying the Word. Likely, any readers who have made it to this point in our book belong to the former category, for even owning this book shows an interest in diving deeply into the Word of God, "rightly dividing" it and "showing themselves approved" (2 Timothy 2:15). That said, we openly acknowledge that not every one of our readers will agree with our interpretation of Revelation, even if they follow our same interpretational methodology. The boundaries around each method, scholars acknowledge, "are difficult to classify. History is messy, and most prophetic movements do not consult with theologians before putting together their belief systems. Consequently, historians who trace these [interpretational] movements over time often find it very difficult to fit them into neat categories."[10] Therefore, we hope the brothers and sisters who don't agree with our approach are as willing as we are to continue being a part of God's community alongside each other despite our differences.

One last thought before we continue: Just as futurists fall into three main subgroups, premillennialists fall mostly into two subgroups: historical premillennialists and dispensational premillennialists. There are a number of differences between these two labels (including the question of when the Church actually started—Old Testament or New—but note that until the events recorded in Genesis 12, "Jews" were not in existence), but the main variation that tends to come up early on regards the Rapture of the saints. From there, interpretational differences include those centering on concepts of the afterlife, the Millennium, and the resurrection of the saints.

Historical premillennialism is closer to what the early Church (heavily influenced by Judaism) believed, including most of the Church fathers (but note that by the fourth century, because of the influence of the Roman Catholic Church, amillenialism arose as a major movement). The Church will be here on earth during the Tribulation and will be rewarded for its faithful service afterward at the Second Advent (post-Tribulation view; frequently shortened to "post-Trib"). For most historical premillennialists, the Millennial Reign is a literal reign, while reference to it lasting a thousand years can be figurative language describing a very lengthy time. This method navigates the Old Testament treatment of the Tribulation and the Millennium and compares it to concepts of the New Temple using the Major Prophets' words regarding the restoration of Israel: Isaiah, Jeremiah, and Ezekiel pronounced judgment on both pagan nations and Judah, building up to themes such as return from exile, universal domination, and the New Temple.

From *A Case for Historic Premillennialism: An Alternative to "Left Behind" Eschatology*—a collaborative effort by several scholars—an "X is Y" formula is introduced as necessary to justify any kind of allegory within the historical premillennial method: If the text directly states something (X) is something else (Y), it can be allegory, while any other language must be interpreted as literal. Using the "dry bones" example from Ezekiel 37, the bones (X) were interpreted directly within the text to be the house of Israel (Y). In that case, the bones are allegory, while everything else is literal, such as the New Temple in Ezekiel 40–43.[11] The post-exile community of Ezekiel's readers didn't interpret the promised Temple restoration as a metaphor, and neither should contemporaries, these scholars say. The removal of God's presence from the old Temple in Ezekiel was literal, so the last Temple, and all of its descriptions, would be also, suggesting that God personally restores the Old Covenant with His people, Israel, in the last days. The problem with such an approach is that, in Revelation 21:22, the Temple *is* God and the Lamb. When asked for answers to this conundrum, one scholar who contributed to *A Case for Historic Premillennialism*, Richard Hess, states that he "cannot easily harmonize the two streams of teaching in the New Testament."[12] Rather than to see this "God and Lamb" Temple-speak from Revelation as possible evidence that any eschatological temple/Temple is allegorical or figurative fulfillment through only the power and presence of God (or that a literal temple on earth could be some kind of end-time trickery by Antichrist), he inadequately and inexplicably maintains his trail of proof that the Old Testament Temple will be restored during the Millennium even though he can't "harmonize" that with the New Testament. (We are not suggesting this is the approach of all historical premillennials. We do, however, see this same kind of interpretational hiccups in a lot of their arguments.)

Scholars of this method draw many conclusions from ancient Jewish writings, wherein the "messianic age" (a sort of Millennium interpretation) is followed by such concepts as the raising of the dead and the afterlife—though interpretations of timeline range from "forty to seven thousand years."[13] Despite this dramatic variation, these texts, as these scholars interpret, collectively teach that this time of peace will be immediately preceded by suffering, so Christ's return is premillennial, but the Rapture is post-Tribulational. To get to these conclusions, many extrabiblical Jewish writings—texts from Intertestamental Period, rabbinic literature from the patristic age, and even later Jewish texts—are consulted. Whereas this may appear to be a fair approach, Helene Dallaire (another collaborator in the aforementioned book) admits that a single, collective Jewish teaching on any of these themes is not possible, as her entire chapter has shown that very few of these ancient documents agree.[14]

In further support of these conclusions (that some would understandably find confusing), collaborator and editor of the work, Craig Blomberg, explains that, according to Jewish apocalyptic literature (1 Enoch, 4 Ezra, 2 Baruch, and the War Scroll of Qumran), the whole reason for the Messiah's return is to "intervene and save his people from unprecedented distress in this world," which is the Tribulation,[15] suggesting that the Church will be on the earth at that time. Blomberg expresses that the 144,000 (from Revelation 7:1–8) are "servants of God" (generically) who are on earth during the Tribulation.[16] Paul's use of "tribulation" in Colossians 1:24 *may*, Blomberg states, allude to "a fixed amount of suffering" for Christians just before the Messiah's return. The parable of the sower (Matthew 13:21; Mark 4:17) can be interpreted as the Tribulation for Christians, as can the Olivet Discourse (Matthew 24:9–29; Mark 13:19–24). Blomberg believes the word "tribulation" is used in Acts 11:19 to refer to the diaspora and persecution of Christians, and in Acts 14:22, Christians must endure Tribulation to enter the Kingdom of God.[17] Blomberg draws from these teachings (and others we won't include because of space limitations) that the Tribulation began at the desecration of the Temple in AD 70 and will end at His Second Coming; therefore, any possible pretribulational Rapture would have to have occurred before AD 70.[18]

Later on, scholar Sung Wook Chung continues the case for historic premillennialism by proposing an alternative reading of Genesis 1–2 to show that earth was a "kingdom" from the beginning. In Genesis 1:26–28, humanity is created in the image of God as "vice-regents" with dominion over the earth, which is their "kingdom" of the "reign of God on the earth."[19] Chung maintains that "Eden" was God's first "temple." The dominion God gave Adam was "physical/kingly." Therefore, the Covenant between God and Abraham shares this literal, physical nature. The messianic prophecy of Genesis 3:15 thereby points to restoration of the dominion-kingdom that was lost at the Fall of man. This restoration will occur through the "last Adam" in the literal Millennial Reign.[20]

Whereas we find this book and others like it to make a few compelling arguments that challenge the thinking of the dispensationalist, we don't believe the matter is irrefutably settled.

Dispensational premillennialism claims that Christ will return before the Millennium, and the Church will be raptured away before the seven-year period known as the Tribulation. It also holds to a literal interpretation of Scripture, or, as one end-times writer from another collaborative work coins, a "normal use of hermeneutics."[21] In this method, there are seven epochs of time known as "dispensations," and we are currently in the sixth (the seventh is the Millennial Reign that follows the Second Advent). For most dispensationalists, the Millennial Reign is literal, as well as one thousand years long.

Since Jesus was the literal fulfillment of Old-Testament prophecy regarding the Messiah, prophecies referring to His return and His Millennial Reign should be expected to be literally fulfilled as well, cancelling the over-spiritualized amillennialism. (This also allows for 2 Peter 1:20–21 to guide us when it states that no prophecy ever originated from within a prophet's own understanding or interpretation.) As we mentioned prior, the dispensationalist sees that Revelation 6–18 shows events getting worse before Jesus' return, and 2 Timothy 3:1–7 also describes the increase in terrible events, cancelling postmillennialism.

One feature of dispensational premillennialism is that it maintains "a sharp and clear distinction between Israel and the church,"[22] meaning that God would have two separate, spiritual-redemption plans for two people groups in the last days. These scholars also believe that Scriptures in the Old Testament pointing to the Millennial Kingdom (Daniel 2:34–35, 44; Isaiah 2:2–4; and Micah 4:1–8) are literal, while the New Testament adds confirmation to these ideas (Luke 1:32–33; Matthew 24:1–25:46; Revelation 20). Therefore, dispensationalists say, the Millennium will play out differently for Israel/Jews than it will for Christians. The New Covenant in Jeremiah 31:31–33 was distinctly (and again literally) made with Judah, or Israel, and not Christians. God's promises about the restoration of the land, Temple, and worship system as defined in Ezekiel 40:1–48:35 must be fulfilled in the manner described—which would not refer to Christians, since Jesus was the one Sacrifice for all.

However, this view is evolving, as many contemporary scholars acknowledge that dispensationalism is beginning to allow "greater continuity between the Testaments" than before.[23] This hybrid dispensationalism (sometimes categorized under the term "progressive dispensationalism") maintains a premillennial timeline with a pre-Tribulation Rapture doctrine, but allows for the merger of the Church with Israel in God's ultimate plan. This approach "has preserved many valuable insights from traditional [or classic] dispensational readings of Scripture," while avoiding the pitfall of splitting them "into irreconcilable [end-time] programs."[24]

Dispensational premillennialism was not widely taught in Church history until the nineteenth century (as heavily introduced by John Nelson Darby of the Plymouth Brethren at the third Powerscourt Conference in 1833), but arriving late in the interpretive game doesn't necessarily make all of its theology wrong. As many researchers into the background of eschatological subjects will concur, the early Church was so focused on establishing who and what Jesus was (refer back to the section "Where and How Some Went Wrong," wherein we illustrated that so much focus of the first three or four centuries was upon the hypostatic union between Father and Son) that the Millennium and the Rapture took a back seat in scholarly discussion. The early Church fathers were, for the most part, unanimously premillennial, so nobody really challenged that area, and the pre-Trib/post-Trib (and the other "Trib" stances) were not discussed until far later. Even after the Protestant Reformation, when a new and more successful platform was established upon which theologians could "challenge the hierarchy" and produce fresh exegesis of Scripture, the entire Church was so entrenched in and occupied with proving or refuting Roman Catholic doctrines and practices like the sale of indulgences and so on that Rapture timing was, again, not a priority.[25] When Christendom finally did calm down enough to tackle a discussion about Rapture timing and other theological issues formerly considered marginal, dispensationalism came a few centuries later, so it's not alarmingly "young in the game," all things considered. It took three centuries *just* to decide what "substance" Christ was, so in this case, the race to "who got there first" is even less important than it normally is.

As for which of these two groups *we* belong to, we tend to lean toward dispensational, pre-Trib premillennialism, but we don't agree on every conclusion it has drawn. For instance, let's look at the idea that the Old Covenant will be restored *by God* for Israel in every literal way, including the priesthood, customs, and animal sacrifices of the Jews in the Old Testament. The main problem we have with this is trying to comprehend why, when Jesus was the ultimate Sacrifice for all, there would ever need to be a return to the former system...? Darby's teachings, solidified circa 1840, maintained God's "two peoples" and "two plans" theology—"the Church" and "Israel" being given different covenantal treatment in the end times—and God could only restore Israel after the Rapture of the Church saints. However, we admit that his "two peoples" and "restoration of Israel" reasoning for this division is suspect as there is little biblical evidence to suggest that God has two separate plans for His followers. (See Hebrews 9:28;

10:3–4, 12, 14 for an absolute and outright refutation of this idea.) Rather, we believe the literal Temple of the Jews *will* be restored…but that it will be a tool for mass deception by Antichrist and it will be *replaced by* the plan of God throughout the Millennial Kingdom and in the New Temple, not because God has "two peoples" and there-fore "two redemptive plans regarding them." (Antichrist will defile the Temple of the Jews in the end times, suggesting that before that moment, politically and socially, he has much clout in the religious establishment of that day, including the support of the Jews' religion and worship practices.) This is only one area where our interpreta-tions of prophetic opinion places us in a minority "hybrid" group all our own.

But that's not to say that such an approach is irresponsible, or that it means we don't know what camp we belong to—and we note this for the benefit of others out there (including you?) who also read a lot of eschatological materials and find that there are flaws in each of them. The more we study the mysteries of Revelation, the more we realize that a scholar could have a hundred doctorates in theology and still be challenged by the words of John's visions we're about to dive into. We are absolute futurist premillennials, but when it comes to historical versus dispensational, pre-Trib versus post-Trib, and so on, there are arguments from almost all sides that we find to be convinc-ing alongside many interpretations that "cheat" Scripture to arrive at their clean conclusions, so we are choosing not to draw any hard lines around a particular group in which we belong where this is concerned.

(A funny title that probably started out as a joke back in the 1980s or so is "pan-Trib," so named after the phrase, "It will all pan out in the end." Also, the prefix "pan" means "all," so, more elaborately, the phrase could be "I respect all tribulational theories." It has gained so much momentum that, today, there are "pan-Tribbers" all over the globe, including some of us. This stance doesn't excuse irresponsibil-ity or indicate a lack of interest in the Word of God; rather, the label helps unite two communities—pre-Tribbers and post-Tribbers—that have been historically warring for dominance since the rise of dispensationalist theology in the nineteenth century. [The "mid-Tribulation" view, as the name suggests, asserts that the Rapture will occur at the middle of the Tribulation, right about the time Antichrist defaults on all his promises to Israel. There is another view that is less common but equally fascinating called "pre-wrath," which positions the Rapture directly prior to the moment that God's supreme wrath is poured out upon the earth. What precise moment that is referring to varies depending on the speaker, but most often these folks believe the "great day of…wrath" from Revelation 6:17 is that fateful instant that occurs just between the last seal and the first trumpet.] In the end, we will see who is right and who is wrong when it all plays out. Meanwhile, personal "pet theologies" that cause strife or division among believers are simply not worth it any more than investigating the subject of "food offered to idols" to the embarrassment of fellow brothers was worth it in Paul's day. We may personally prefer the pre-Trib side of the issue theologically, as it makes the most sense to us, but we are also happy to accept a pan-Tribber position socially.)

That said, we'll just share a couple of pre-Trib thoughts in case some readers are new to the concept and find the Tribulation terrifying (just two verses, we promise).

1. First Thessalonians 5:9a directly states about believers: "For God hath not appointed us to wrath." If God didn't appoint us for His wrath, why would we be here on earth when His extreme wrath will fall upon everyone during the Tribulation? This question gets even meatier when we consider that the whole purpose of the Tribulation is to give everyone on earth one final chance to turn to God. Why would that apply to believers who have already given their lives to God? According to many interpreters who specialize in the timing of Revelation events, the Church will be experiencing certain things during the Tribulation, such as the Marriage Supper of the Lamb,

supporting the idea that we would be gone by the start of the Tribulation. (Support for this idea is partly found in the order of events. The Marriage Supper of the Lamb, involving all saints together, takes place in Revelation 19:7–9, and *then* Christ comes to establish the Millennial Reign in Revelation 19:11–20. How could He have this Supper without us, the saints, who are the subject of this feast, if we are on earth suffering at the time?)

2. In Revelation 3:10 (in the letter to the church in Philadelphia), Christ states: "Because thou hast kept the word of my patience, I also will keep thee from the hour of temptation, which shall come upon all the world, to try them that dwell upon the earth." Initially, this English rendering makes it sound like Jesus is going to keep people from being tempted. The "hour of temptation" is frequently (and for good reason) translated as "the hour of trial." The Greek word used here, *peirasmos*, can be translated "temptation," but first and foremost, in this context, the word means "trial, probation, testing, being tried."[26] It is derived from another Greek word, *peirazo*, which scholars collectively acknowledge to state: "*I make trial of, try, test...* God *tests* man by means of suffering or in some other way."[27] More accurately, then, Christ is here promising to "keep" His followers from "the hour of trial" that will come "upon all the world," the folks who are "upon the earth," as it pertains to how God will "test man by means of suffering." Who is He keeping from having to suffer the trials upon the earth in that hour if His plan is not to Rapture the saints *before* the Tribulation? That His promise here would only apply to the Christians in Philadelphia is unreasonable, because the blessings and warnings of the letters to the seven churches of Revelation are unanimously agreed among academics to be relevant to all people of all time. Some believe the true intent of His words were that He intends to "protect" believers dur-

ing that time, but if that's the case, why did He mince words? Why wouldn't He just say "protect during" instead of "keep thee *from*"? And lastly, He didn't only say He would "keep thee from trial," He specifically said "the hour of," which denotes a specific time period (a key element of eschatology that further supports that the Tribulation is in view here).

It's food for thought, anyway…

But, in addition to offering a crash-course, two-verse reflection on behalf of the pre-Trib theology for those seeking reassurance, we shared our leaning to make a very important point: There are certainly wonderful, sincere pre-Tribbers who are very concerned with what happens to people after they are raptured away, as they believe they will be. However, for other pre-Tribbers, there tends to be a self-righteous attitude that permeates their faith in this one area, making them somewhat Pharisaic in their ministry to others. These are the folks who say, "What do I care what happens after I'm gone? People had their chance to accept Christ and they didn't, so now they will suffer. The issue of the Tribulation regarding [fill-in-the-blank event] doesn't matter to me anyway, because I'm not going to be here. I'll be with Jesus in the clouds." We can sit down with a fellow believer and agree on *every one* of their eschatological conclusions, and still feel as if we have little in common with them if this is their callous approach to those who remain. The Great Commission of Christ was paramount to what makes the Church His Family. If we start watching the signs of the times and find ourselves to be "the enlightened ones"—who can't be troubled to truly care and pray for those who will go through the most intense suffering in human history—we have no business calling ourselves followers of the Man who *demanded* that His people love the lost.

If you're pre-Trib, we challenge you: Look for every opportunity you can for the works of your life to outlive you. If the Rapture *does* take all the saints from the world, that event will be a message to the lost in itself, but those who are still on earth will only have what remains of your ministry (and of others) after you're gone to help them find and come to know the precious Yeshua. Assuming you are willing to live your life today as if it will affect your grandchildren, as most likely do, then live as though everything you do will be presented to a future generation of souls who matter just as much to God as your own family. For we will not know the hour of Christ's return, and we must be ready always: "Therefore, beloved, since you are waiting for these, be diligent to be found by him without spot or blemish" (2 Peter 3:14).

Quick Note Regarding Sources

Going forward, part of our research centers on several works from renowned Revelation expert and theologian, Gregory K. Beale. Though he has been described by others in the field as personally belonging to amillennial leanings, of all the multiple studies out there on Revelation, his wholly unbiased approach is the most thorough. It encompasses, quite exhaustively, the numerous methodologies that have been raised throughout Church history from every known interpretational angle, discussing the strengths and/or weaknesses of each opinion. Because of his in-depth, systematic breakdowns and immense knowledge of ancient languages and culture, alongside his frequently neutral treatment of all passages, his collection has been championed as both a fair and meticulous visit into Revelation by many, including the well-known ancient Hebrew and Greek theologian, Dr. Michael Heiser. We believe, for this reason and many others (such as his willingness to consider extrabiblical documents relating to some subjects in Revelation), Beale is a responsible first (but not only) source for us to consult regarding the harder passages.

A few other sources we've found immensely helpful are Jamieson, Fausset, & Brown's *Commentary Critical and Explanatory on the Whole Bible*; Albert Barnes' *Barnes' Notes*; Kendall Easley's *Revelation:*

Volume 12; Bruce Barton's *Revelation*; and Leon Morris' *Revelation: An Introduction and Commentary: Volume 20*.

We will now turn to the common symbols and their most frequently assigned meanings, followed by a short analysis of the sequence of judgments, and then the body of the text within Revelation.

Common Symbols

Because of Revelation's extensive use of numbers and symbols, it's easy to get lost in what means what in this apocalyptic book. Though the following list isn't necessarily every premillennial scholar's opinion, generally, folks in the academic world agree on the following list of symbols and their meanings (or what they link to). It's a good idea to get familiar with these now, and to bookmark them for reference later (but note that we clarify them as we go along, too):

Numbers (in numerical order, whether literal or not):

- **One:** certain special use is capitalized in many translations; often refers to God and infers the union of the Trinity
- **Two:** indicates confirmation (like Old Testament rules of "two witnesses" and so on)
- **Three:** Trinity
- **Four:** the earth
- **Six:** the number of man; evil
- **Seven:** the number of God; goodness; divine confirmation, fullness, or completion; sometimes meaning "infinite"
- **Ten:** politics or political completion; the rule of man; man's government; often relating to the Man of Sin in charge over man's government
- **Twelve:** another number of God relating to the twelve tribes of Israel, the twelve apostles, and their relation to sacred items or

images; also, like "seven," relating to divine confirmation, fullness, or completion, but this time in regard to God's ultimate and final plan

- **One quarter/one-third:** measurement of judgment
- **Three and a half:** half of seven; midway point of the Tribulation; temporary circumstances
- **Ten thousand:** the largest number in Koine Greek (without having to add) representing an indefinitely large amount or number; can translate to "myriad"
- **One hundred forty-four thousand:** the number of the elect people of God, based on twelve thousand times twelve (therefore possibly meaning "complete")
- **Two hundred million:** representing the number of people alive on earth (figurative language of John's time); can translate to "two myriads of myriads"

Animals:

- **Lion/Lamb:** capitalized in many translations; always refers to Jesus
- **Wild beasts:** Antichrist; False Prophet
- **Frogs:** demons
- **Horses:** military power; invasion

Colors:

- **Black:** chaos; tragedy; disaster; misfortune
- **Red:** war; blood; violence
- **Scarlet:** royalty; luxury; immoral, immodest, or shameful
- **Purple:** divine royalty; extravagance
- **Gold:** royalty; glory; brilliance; magnificence
- **Pale/pale green:** death; mortality; plagues; sickness

- **White:** cleanliness; washed clean; purity; something/someone ancient or ancient wisdom
- **Green/Emerald:** rest; relaxation; rejuvenation; something refreshing

Characters:

- **Alpha and Omega:** literally, the "alpha" is the first letter of the Greek alphabet and the "omega" is the last letter; representing God as the "First and the Last" eternal authority and comprehension of, and over, all earthly things
- **Harlot** [sometimes "whore"] **of Babylon:** false religion; one-world superchurch of Antichrist; the one the Beast devours
- **Angel(s):** messenger(s) of God who carries out His commands and the events of the book
- **Woman:** people; cities/regions that represents certain people groups (like Israel being known as a "she")
- **Bride/Bride of the Lamb:** matrimonial term representing the people of God, the Church, and, some say, the New Jerusalem
- **Seven churches:** literal churches active in Asia Minor at the time Revelation was written; today their warnings and messages are directed to the contemporary Church universal
- **Twenty-four elders:** first, as members of the heavenly court; second, as the addition of the twelve tribes to the twelve apostles; third, some say "people of God," generally, as is represented by the twelve tribes and twelve apostles in history
- **Antichrist:** Man of Sin; literally the one who appears "opposite of" and/or "instead of" Christ (terminology discussed later), resembling Jesus and His works but from wicked, evil motives to deceive; the great politician who establishes both his one-world order and one-world religion
- **Dragon:** Satan; some say the "ancient serpent"

Places:

- **Babylon:** "city" (or territories) of wicked, evil people, belonging to the Man of Sin
- **Jerusalem/New Jerusalem:** "city" (or territories) of good, righteous, and faithful people who belong to God
- **Sodom:** in context of Revelation: less of a "place" and more of a symbol of rebellion/hostility against God (as the Sodomites of the Old Testament were); symbol of apostasy (see: Deuteronomy 32:32; Isaiah 1:9; Ezekiel 16:46, 49, 55; Jeremiah 23:14)
- **Egypt:** like "Sodom," less of a "place" and more a symbol of rebellion/hostility against God and His purposes or plans (as the Egyptians of the Old Testament were)
- **The sea:** symbolic habitation of evil and destructive forces; "sea of humanity"
- **Armageddon:** location of the final showdown between good and evil

Miscellaneous:

- **Crowns/coronets/diadems (or other headdresses related to royalty):** royal authority and/or power
- **Thrones:** royalty; authority
- **Heads and horns:** kings; rulers; power; authority; sometimes a kingdom
- **Sword:** judgment of God; Word of God
- **Robes/long robes:** priesthood; priests
- **Eyes:** knowledge
- **Palms:** victory
- **Wings:** mobility; fastness or swiftness; omnipresence of God
- **Lampstands:** the seven churches of Asia Minor; by extension, the Church universal and/or Israel's faithful

- **Seals:** fixtures on the scroll representing the contract of mankind's redemption; the first of three judgment series
- **Trumpets:** instrument representing the announcement of an event (possibly also the voice of God as opposed to a literal trumpet blast); the second of three series of judgments
- **Bowls that "pour out":** represents the vessels that pour down the third and final of the three judgment series of God

Judgments: Parallel or Sequential?

The judgments in the book of Revelation are represented by the last three common symbols identified in the previous section. Each judgment is a set of seven, representing a series. In the order in which John described them, they are: 1) seven seal judgments; 2) seven trumpet judgments; and 3) seven bowl judgments.

A nearly never-ending hermeneutical debate is whether or not all three of these series are simply "retellings" of the same judgment three times (parallel), or if they are three complete and different sets of judgments, one set leading directly into the next (sequential). Some believe it's a mixture, wherein some of the seals are also trumpets, some of the trumpets are also bowls, and so on.

To illustrate how parallelism works, we will use a very old and familiar example you will probably recognize: Imagine three blind men approaching an elephant. The first outstretches his hands, takes hold of a leg, and after feeling the rough skin, concludes that it is the trunk of a tree. The second touches the side of the animal, believing it to be a rough wall. The third lets his hands roll down the tail and announces that it's a rope with a frayed tip. (Other versions involve different imagery, such as the idea that the tail is a broom, the tusk is a smooth spear, and so on.) All three men felt the same animal, and all of their reports were true according to what they experienced, but because they could not see what they were touching, none could accurately describe the full reality of the elephant.

John the Revelator was given special sight into the end times through Jesus, personally (Revelation 1:1). But because these are prophecies of things to come, and no prophet draws from his own understanding regarding the fulfillments (2 Peter 1:20), John could both a) report the truth honestly according to what he saw; while b) reporting the same events telling different details each time he sees it—like a blind man being led from an elephant's trunk to its side, or whatever combination. From the parallel perspective, there could be a judgment from the "seals" series that overlaps a judgment from the "trumpets" series, and so on, even when that telling involves slightly different details in Scripture. In other words, though there are differences, they are not contradictory.

However, because there are very real differences between the judgments series, some prefer to adopt the sequential model: the seven seals occur, *then* the seven trumpets, *then* the seven bowls, totaling twenty-one distinct events.

There is evidence to support both sides of this debate. We authors personally believe that what is being described in the seal judgments is conspicuously different from the other two series, while we admit that the trumpet judgments bear a remarkable similarity to the bowl judgments. For instance, the second trumpet involves a "mountain" being thrown into the sea, and the second bowl reports that everything in the seas die. The third trumpet states that many people die from the bitter waters, while the third bowl details rivers and springs turning to "blood."

Focusing only on the trumpets and bowls to decipher whether they are parallel or sequential, perhaps the place to start is not to compare how judgment series are *similar*, but how they are *different* in their effect on people and how each event plays out. From that approach, 1) the trumpets only affect part of the population, while the bowl plagues are global; 2) humanity's repentance appears to be a significant response to the trumpets, while the narrative of the bowls reports that humanity curses God (Revelation 11:21); 3) the first four trumpets do affect the inhabitants of the earth, but only indirectly, as the judgments are carried out upon the *earth*, while the bowls launch into a direct attack upon those who take the mark of the Beast (16:2); 4) the effects of the trumpet series appear to be more gradual than those of the bowl series, which read like a rapid outbreak of one judgment after another; 5) the similarities are not enough to cancel the divergent descriptions—for example, the fourth trumpet and fourth bowl both affect the sun, but the trumpet darkens a third of the sun while the bowl describes the sun scorching people on the earth; 6) a sequential description allows the natural reading that the judgments increase in their intensity; and 7) the trumpets could lead to what happens with the bowls, making them related but distinct (the second trumpet's "mountain" thrown into the sea could *cause* the second bowl's conclusion that everything in the seas die).

As for our personal opinion: We have no problem allowing the three series to be sequential (therefore separate), not only because of the distinct differences just listed, but also because we believe God is supremely loving and will give as many "last chances" as possible before the end. That said, we acknowledge that the varying parallel theories are legitimate and responsible, so our approach in the coming chapters will be to cover the events in the order John lists them, without any intent to aggressively teach sequential-judgment theology.

Speaking of parallelism: For space reasons, we will not be addressing how some of the judgments are an outright reflection of a number of plagues upon the Egyptians in the Exodus account, as that discussion can get lengthy. We do, however, encourage you to open your Bible and do your own comparative study. It's clear that the God who punished the Egyptians is the same God who rains His judgment down heavily in the end times, and for similar reasons (persecution of His people and corporate, pagan rejection of Him). Though this is a fascinating trail, it opens up other theologies that branch off into deep, Old-Testament dialogue, so we are foregoing the temptation to lay out all the similarities at length. Likewise, though the book of Revelation is intrinsically tied to certain books of the Old Testament (Daniel, for example)—and though we reference those texts quite often—we do not plan to go into as much comparative details as some works do. Our purpose in the conversation of Revelation's contemporary relevance is to show what John said and how he said it, using other books and evidence to support or clarify his prophetic narrative regarding future judgments, *not* to launch into a bottomless theological discourse on every verse. This book points to Jesus, primarily, so we build to that climax, hoping to offer a basic overview that serves as a) an approachable outline for newer readers/believers, and b) a helpful reminder for mature readers/believers.

Finally, let's get into the book of Revelation itself. When we are finished, please *do not* skip the ending… This book closes with a powerful exhortation of Christian action.

REVELATION

We have discussed the book's setting, audience, occasion, interpretational methods, common symbols, and parallel vs. sequential approaches to the judgments. With that behind us, we are ready to begin the exciting words from Christ to John regarding our future.

Jesus' Appearance to John (Revelation 1)

JOHN OPENS HIS DOCUMENT with the paramount statement that this book is "the Revelation of Jesus Christ" (Revelation 1:1). This is an important disclosure, as it immediately notifies the reader that all of the content to follow (for the next twenty-two chapters—Revelation's total length) was not only written through the guidance of the Spirit, like the rest of Scripture, but that it was delivered directly from the Risen Messiah.

John further explains that this Revelation of Christ was given to the Messiah by God to show His "angels" (or "servants") what is coming "soon." Christ then sent an angel to present the message to John, the servant of God who therefore recorded what he saw. Then John states that the one who reads this book to the Church, and the one who listens to it and obeys it, will experience a blessing, for the time of the document's fulfillment is nigh (1:1–3). (Scholars have marveled throughout the centuries at this declaration, as this is the only book of the Bible that promises a blessing, in no uncertain terms, for those who read it, obey it, and tell others about it. Many commentaries note that this is probably a central reason Revelation has gotten so much more attention than any other biblical book, because otherwise, its enigmatic nature may have discouraged a lot of folks, including theologians, from tackling it the way they have.)

This early on, some commentators dive in on the word "soon" and find reason to believe that it supports events occurring during John's day. That's not necessarily an irresponsible conclusion based on word studies and grammar, but in the context of biblical literature—wherein God's timing is *not* our timing (Psalm 90:4; 2 Peter 3:8)—"soon" should stress the importance of "readiness" on behalf of the recipients as opposed to a rapid fulfillment within history. This language is paramount behind the doctrine of the "imminency" of Christ's Second Advent ("imminent," meaning "could happen any moment"). As Revelation was likely written in AD 95, then from AD 95 *forward* (not representing events of Jerusalem's destruction in AD 70), Christ could literally return at any moment, regardless of one's interpretation of signs and worldwide events. (This can add further evidence in support of pretribulational Rapture and premillennial Advent timing. For if Christ's return was *posttribulational*, we wouldn't have need to "watch the signs"; we would merely watch as the Tribulation plays out and count down to an identified time of return, which the Bible refutes with language regarding Jesus coming "like a thief in the night" [Matthew 24:36–44, 1 Thessalonians 5:1–3, 2 Peter 3:10, Revelation 3:3].)

Between the short introduction and the coming letters to the seven churches individually, John writes a salutation from his own voice to all of the seven churches in the province of Asia. He wishes them grace and peace from the One who was, is, and is yet to come, from the "sevenfold" Spirit of God and Christ. Jesus Christ is the Faithful Witness of these things, as the first to rise from the dead, and as the ruler over the world. All glory and power forever goes to Him whose blood was shed for our benefit; He has turned us into a Kingdom of priests for God, the Father (1:4–6). (According to Beale, the "sevenfold" Spirit, or "seven spirits" in some translations, represents fullness and completion, not "seven entities" or "archangels," as some suppose from ancient, apocryphal or extrabiblical Jewish literature.[28])

Jesus is going to come with the clouds of heaven, and *all* will see Him, including those who contributed to His death, and all nations "shall wail" because of Him—even so, "Amen" (a word meaning "we agree"; 1:7).

There has been some confusion about this statement. Commentators note that it initially seems "un-Christian" for John to write a hearty "amen" at the idea that everyone will "wail." Likewise, the "all" is a little confusing, considering that the sight of Jesus would assumedly be a joyful thing for believers. *Jamieson, Fausset, & Brown* sheds some light on this moment, explaining that this reference to "all" includes "the unconverted at the general judgment; and especially at His pre-millennial advent, the Antichristian confederacy (Zec 12:3–6, 9; 14:1–4; Mt 24:30).... Even the godly while rejoicing in His love shall feel penitential sorrow at their sins, which shall all be manifested at the general judgment."[29] This is a moment in which an "amen" is no longer out of place, because the consummation of God's plan and His vindication are about to be realized in these texts. John, an apostle driven by passionate zeal for the lost in all his other writings, therefore would not have said "amen" to the suffering of people, but to God's plan on earth being carried out in the interest of the lost and vindication of the saved, finally.

John goes on to write that Jesus says He is the Alpha and Omega, the First and the Last, the Beginning and the End, who is, always was, and is still to come—the Almighty One (1:8).

John is, to these churches, a brother and fellow partner in suffering for the Kingdom, enduring alongside them in patience in and endurance of what Jesus has called His people to do. Because of John's boldness in sharing his personal testimony and preaching about the Name of Christ, he was exiled to the island of Patmos. On the "Lord's day" (a Sunday, as the Greek from the second century on suggests), John was worshipping in the Spirit, when suddenly, he heard a voice from behind him as loud as a trumpet blast. The voice instructed him to write down everything he was about to see and send it to the seven churches in Ephesus, Smyrna, Pergamum, Thyatira, Sardis, Philadelphia, and Laodicea (1:9–11).

When John turned to see who was speaking to him, he saw seven golden candlesticks (more often, "lampstands," representing the seven churches; now the fullness of the Church universal). In the middle of these was the Son of Man, wearing a long robe with a golden sash that ran across the width of His chest. The Son of Man's hair was white like wool or snow, and His eyes looked like flames of fire. His feet were like bronze that had been refined in a fire (meaning purified—Jesus is a wholly "pure" being; see similar treatment in Revelation 3:18). His voice thundered like the waves of the ocean. He held seven stars (representing the "angels" of the seven churches; more on this in a moment) in His right hand. From His mouth came a sharp, two-edged sword (the Word; judgment of God against His [and our] enemies). And His face shone like the brilliant sun (similar to the description of Stephen, whose face shone like the sun as he saw Christ at the right hand of the Father during his stoning event; this signifies majestic connection to God).

This depiction of the Son of Man in Revelation 1:12–16 was used of the Ancient of Days in the Old Testament. In the New Testament, it is of Jesus—titled after, and described nearly identically to, what Daniel saw in his prophetic vision (see Daniel 7:9–13; 10:6; 12:3, 6–7). (For more on "lampstands" or "stars," see Zechariah 4 and Daniel 12:3; for "sharp, two-edged sword," see Isaiah 11:4; 49:2.)

When John saw Him, he fell at His feet as if he were dead. But the Son of Man laid His hand on John and told him not to be afraid, for He was the First and Last, the Living One, who died but was now alive forever, and who holds "the keys of hell and of death" (He has authority over death and the grave). Jesus then instructs John to write down "the things which thou hast seen, and the things which are, and the things which shall be hereafter," and then Christ self-interprets what John is seeing: "The mystery of the seven stars which thou sawest in my right hand, and the seven golden candlesticks [or "lampstands"]. The seven stars are the angels of the seven churches: and the seven candlesticks which thou sawest are the seven churches" (Revelation 1:17–20).

Seven Letters to Seven Churches (Revelation 2-3)

FROM THE BEGINNING of chapter 2 through the end of chapter 3, John writes Jesus' messages to the seven churches of Asia Minor. Again, these churches were literal, historical assemblies in John's day, but the advice Christ gave them through His servant John are given to the whole Church Body today, just like the Epistles. Each of the letters begins with Christ's words, "To the angel of [church name], write..."

"Angel" here comes from the Greek word *angelos*, which literally translates "messenger." Scholars have never agreed about whether the letters are being addressed to human messengers or to heavenly angels, as the word can, and has, appeared in the Bible in reference to either kind of being that's sent on an assignment. For instance, John the Baptist was referred to as an *angelos* in Matthew 11:10, and we know he was human. As Beale notes, this designation could refer to any one of four possible meanings: 1) simply angels; 2) angels who are spiritual representatives of the churches (like assigned guardians of the unseen realm); 3) human leaders of the churches, like bishops, pastors, or deacons; or 4) personifications of the churches' spirit or character.[30] After explaining this and digging into evidence from a great number of sources, Beale believes literal "angels" are in view, while the authors of *Jamieson, Fausset, & Brown*, with an equally convincing argument, believe this refers to "bishops."

John is here instructed to "write letters," and we have no indication that they aren't literal, physical, handwritten letters, so the idea that he would then hand them over to angels is a bit puzzling. It's hard to imagine it would be standard behavior that one of these churches would hear a knock at the door and open it to see a celestial being in all his glory appearing on its doorstep just to deliver some mail from Patmos. On the other hand, it's totally believable. Considering the content of this book and the importance it would have to the early Church, having correspondence hand-delivered by an angelic messenger from heaven would certainly invoke more awe than would a human messenger, compelling the churches to take the words from Christ more seriously. This is the same day and age when, as seen in the Epistles, anyone could come with "dreams" or "visions" and teach whatever they wanted, claiming they had a message from God. That's not to say they would have been disbelieving of the illustrious Apostle John in person, but as he was exiled, at the very least the man who brought the mail would claim to have been sent by John, and there's no telling if that would have been accepted seven times in a row (at seven different buildings). It's odd, though, that an event as major as seven angels appearing on or near the same day in seven key churches of Asia Minor would not have been recorded in detail by our trusted historians or Church fathers, which argues for the human-messenger interpretation.

The "fear not" response of angels throughout the Bible also raises initial doubts about the idea that an angel at the door of a church would have looked like a mere mortal, but Hebrews 13:2—acknowledging that we may be "entertaining" heavenly beings "unaware" of what they are—makes that a possibility as well... As much as we wish we could nail this down, for two thousand years, no one has been able to, and far be it for the authors of this book to accomplish what the greatest minds in history could not. We have no choice but to say we are unsure on this issue. That said, though *angelos* appears throughout the Word to mean either "angel" or "human" messenger, it's noteworthy that in the book of Revelation, the overwhelming use is of *heavenly beings*. Therefore, how those deliveries would have gone down and what the reactions of the churches would have been upon receiving them remains a mystery.

What we do know is that, despite the "to the angel...write" opener, scholars unanimously agree that the harsh rebukes of Jesus would not be directed to a heavenly being as recipient. (That would potentially open up an impossible and absurd "fallen angel" theology that is most definitely not intended.) If celestial servants are actually in view here, then it can only mean that they are representatives/guardians of the churches and therefore responsible for overseeing the communication.

The following is a summary of the seven letters. All words are written from Christ's perspective, so the pronoun "I" (along with "My," "Me," etc.) refers to the first-person sentiments of Jesus. Following each is a moment of reflection on its content:

To Ephesus, from the One who holds seven stars in His right hand and walks among the golden lampstands: I am aware of all you do, and I see your patience, endurance, and your suffering for My Name. You've investigated, and exposed, false apostles, refusing to tolerate them. This is very good. But I do have a complaint: The love you had for Me and for each other in the beginning is gone. Look how far you have fallen away from that first love! Turn back to Me. Go back to doing the works you did at first. If you don't repent, I will remove your lampstand from its place among the seven churches. You hate the wickedness of the Nicolaitanes, just as I do, and this speaks in favor of you. Anyone who has ears to hear must use their hearing to listen to the Spirit's message to all the churches: To all who are victorious, I will give them fruit from the Tree of Life in God's Paradise (Revelation 2:1–7).

Reflection: The "Nicolaitanes" are addressed in Irenaeus' *Against Heresies*. He writes that they "are the followers of that Nicolas who was one of the seven first ordained to the diaconate [body of deacons] by the apostles [in Acts 6:3, 5]. They lead lives of unrestrained indulgence. The character of these men is very plainly pointed out in the Apocalypse of John, when they are represented as teaching that it is a matter of indifference to practise adultery."[31] Recall that Ephesus was the prized center of Artemis/Diana worship as well as the Imperial Cult. If Irenaeus is correct, this Nicolas that the apostles first ordained as a deacon of the early Church in Acts was, at some point, given over to the temptations of the flesh and later led fellow Christians into pagan sexual immorality.

Not everyone agrees with this literal interpretation, however. Some, like the authors of *Jamieson, Fausset, & Brown*, compare the meaning of the Greek name, "Nicolaos," ("conqueror of the people") to the same name in Hebrew, *Belang Am*, or "Balaam," meaning "Destroyer of the People."[32] This symbolism of names (and items, colors, etc.) throughout Revelation supports the idea that the Ephesians are here commended for refusing to tolerate a group of people who have adopted the extreme end of antinomianism (the opposite of legalism; such freedom under grace that one is no longer bound to moral absolutes). In short, the spirit of Balaam, as carried by false believers, threatened this church with teachings that a new and progressive Christianity allowed one to hold the title of "Christian," practice the debauchery of the pagans, and at the end of the day, still be considered holy by grace.

This latter meaning of "Nicolaitanes" is the more likely, and it comes into sharper focus as such in the letter to Pergamum.

To Smyrna, from the One who is the First and Last, who was dead but is now alive: I am aware of your suffering and poverty, but you are actually rich! I am also aware of the blasphemy of those who come against you, who say they are Jews, but they cannot be, because they are of the synagogue of Satan. You are about to suffer further, and the devil will even throw some of you into prison as a test, but don't be afraid. You will suffer for ten days, but if you remain faithful even when threatened with death, I will give you the crown of life. Anyone who has ears to hear must use their hearing to listen to the Spirit's message to all the churches: To all who are victorious, you will not be harmed by the second death (Revelation 2:8–11).

Reflection: Note that if the "angel" of this church was human, it was probably Polycarp, a well-known, first-century bishop of Smyrna and celebrated Church father of many denominations who was martyred at the stake (then stabbed when the fire failed).

Smyrna was one of the first cities in Asia Minor to worship the Roman emperor in the Imperial Cult. In addition to its temple of Emperor Tiberius, it housed a temple to Roma, the goddess who personified Rome and demanded compliance to the Roman State. Scholars believe the temple of Roma in Smyrna was the very first in the world.[33] Therefore, the pressure upon the Christians to worship Rome would have been intense enough to lead to imprisonment or worse in this city. As Satan is "the false accuser" (Revelation 12:10), these "false Jews" who opposed these Christians (possibly for not giving in to the demands of the Imperial Cult) made up the "synagogue" of this enemy.

In the "Common Symbols" section, we noted that "ten" is the number of man's government. "Ten days" of suffering is believed by most to refer to a short period of suffering under the government of man, while, in close proximity to a "test," it is also linked to the "ten days" of Daniel's testing (Daniel 1:12–15). Daniel and his three friends were pressured to eat the king's meat that was unclean to them, so they refused, eating only vegetables and drinking only water. In the ancient Near East, sitting and eating in the presence of the king was to swear loyalty to him, and Nebuchadnezzar believed himself to be divine.[34] Thus, we find a parallel between a very early, Babylonian "Imperial Cult" idea in the story of Daniel that connects to the "ten days" of "testing" for the Christians of Smyrna. If they, like Daniel, maintained their faithfulness, they would be given "the crown of life" (eternal life) from Jesus. To the victorious, the "second death" cannot touch them. We read of this term again in Revelation 21:8, where we read that the wicked "shall have their part in the lake which burneth with fire and brimstone: which is the second death."

To Pergamum, from the One with a sharp, two-edged sword: I am aware that you live in the same city where the throne of Satan is stationed, but even then, you have remained loyal to Me, even when Antipas, My witness, was martyred right there in the city of Satan. However, I have a few complaints against you: You tolerate those whose teaching is like Balaam, who caused Israel to stumble by eating meat offered to idols and engaging in sexually immoral acts. Similarly, you have some Nicolaitanes within your assembly who follow the same teaching. Repent of this, or I will appear to you suddenly and fight against these wicked men with the sword of My mouth. Anyone who has ears to hear must use their hearing to listen to the Spirit's message to all the churches: To all who are victorious, I will give manna from heaven, and to each, a white stone with a new name that nobody understands except those who receive it (Revelation 2:12–17).

Reflection: Pergamum, the "city of Satan" where "Satan's throne" was, housed a vast number of pagan temples behind a cone-shaped hill, and both pantheonic worship and Imperial Cult worship were a major focus. Though it wasn't known for its commercial success, its great library (featuring more than two hundred thousand scrolls) became somewhat of a pilgrimage for travelers. The word "parchment" is etymologically linked to the name "Pergamum." Perhaps it was for this reason that it became the capital of the Roman province within the borders of Asia.[35] More likely, however, this city's penchant for venerating Asclepius, Zeus, Dionysus, Demeter, and Athene was what angered Jesus to the point of calling it satanic. Scholars acknowledge that although Asclepius was worshipped all over Rome, this particular location elicited pilgrims from all over the world to "get healed" in Pergamum, and the temple of Zeus—complete with a "throne-like alter"[36]—was the glittering pride of the city. Though scholars are still debating exactly which of these pagan features would have been the "throne" of Satan, as Pergamum was the capital of the province, it was also "the centre of the emperor cult for the whole province."[37] Beal acknowledges that residents of Pergamum called their city the "temple warden" over their imperial god, Caesar, and anyone who refused to worship him would be found guilty of treason against Rome.[38]

Only a single legend of martyrdom told by the Church fathers regarding one named "Antipas" gives us a clue who this "witness" may have been. The commentators of *Jamieson, Fausset, & Brown* note that this "Antipas, in Domitian's reign, was shut up in a red-hot brazen bull, and ended his life in thanksgivings and prayers."[39] Because the other tellings of his end are too graphic to reiterate here, and we aren't completely sure if he's the same man to whom Jesus is referring, this is all we will say of him, though we will note that his intense servitude earned him great and worthy mention by Christ, personally.

The Nicolaitanes and their symbolic association to Balaam is explained formerly in our review of the letter to Ephesus. In this case, Christ threatens to fight against them with His "sword," which is known to be a symbol of truth, judgment, and the Word of God.

John 4:31–34 speaks of a kind of food the disciples didn't know about, and in John 6:25–59, Jesus is the "Bread of Life." Whoever comes to Him will never thirst or be hungry (spiritually speaking). This is likely in mind when this same author (John) hears Jesus' words about a special "manna from heaven."

As far as the "white stones," it may be disappointing to learn that, after centuries of dedicated research, scholars still aren't sure exactly what this means. Of hundreds of possibilities, seven have garnered the most interest, but we will only cover three of those ideas (as we find them more likely than the others). Remember that the color white, in the book of Revelation, is a symbol for purity or something washed clean. And names were crucial in Israel's history, so a secret or unknown name inscribed on a stone appeals to scholars as a personal identity of the believer that is between him and Christ. That is far more exciting to the student who has researched names in antiquity, when a "hidden name was precious" because it stood for the idea that God had instilled within that person a "new character," establishing him as a new person, separated from the old man.[40] Keep this in mind as you read the following theories of what the white stone may have alluded to:

1) During trials of this day, a jury member appealing for acquittal (the release of a prisoner, for example) turned in a white stone as an official statement of his decision. (A black stone was used to state the charge of guilt.) Thus, the stone could mean the blessing of freedom (a reversal of a "guilty verdict") from man's government.

2) Rabbinic traditions from the Midrash state that when manna fell from heaven in the wilderness, it was accompanied by precious stones and pearls. Though Jesus did not endorse or prove this idea in this letter, He *may* have been trumping a tradition that would have been familiar to His readers by offering His own replacement. Interestingly, He just told the believers of Pergamum that He would give them hidden manna from heaven, so if the wilderness manna was found alongside precious stones (or even if that's what the early Christians believed), these two "gifts" from Christ here would fit well together.

3) On the breastplate of the Jewish high priest were twelve jewels, and on each was inscribed a name of one of the twelves tribes. Due to translational difficulties, there is much debate regarding which stone represented what tribes. However, most sources tend to believe that the *Yahalom* stone, considered to be a pearl or diamond (either could be "white" compared to all others) belonged to the tribe of Zebulun. At first, this doesn't appear to mean much, as Jesus and Zebulun are not necessarily linked in any fantastic way, but it is interesting at the very least that Zebulun's tribal territory was what became known in New Testament times as Galilee, precisely where Jesus was from. Isaiah 9:1 prophesied that although God had "humbled" Zebulun in the past, He will one day honor them in Galilee. This messianic

prophecy points to the fact that Jews of the tribe of Zebulun would be some of the first to hear the Gospel (like these early church members!). Additionally, Moses' benediction for the tribe of Zebulun was that its dealings with the Gentiles would be blessed (Deuteronomy 33:18–19), and nobody ever "dealt" with the Gentiles in a more blessed way than Christ. Therefore, this "white stone" *may* be a reference to the breastplate stone of the high priest, but instead of the tribal name "Zebulun," Jesus promises the name will be a blessed one that only has meaning to its wearer. Regardless of Zebulun, any tribal stone could have been in mind here, and the color is insignificant when "white" in Revelation stands for purity, symbolically replacing the need for any other pigment to be present.

To Thyatira, from the Son of God, whose eyes are like flames, and whose feet are like refined bronze: I know all that you are doing. I've witnessed your love, faith, service, patience, and endurance, and I am aware that you are constantly improving in all these areas. But I have a complaint against you: You are allowing that false prophet, that Jezebel, to mislead My people. She teaches them to eat food offered to idols and commit acts of sexual sin. I gave her time to repent, but she will not; she doesn't want to turn away from her immoral ways. So I will throw her onto a bed—her and those who commit adultery with her—and all of them will suffer immensely unless they repent. Even her children will die, and then all the churches will know that I am the One who has the power to search thoughts and intentions within the heart and minds of people. I will give to each of you believers whatever you deserve. But to those who have not followed these teachings, these depths of Satan, I have a message: I ask nothing more of you than for you to hold onto what you have until I come. To all who are victorious and obey Me to the end: I will give them power over all the nations, and they will rule over them with a rod of iron. I will also gift them with the morning star. Anyone who has ears to hear must use their hearing to listen to the Spirit's message to all the churches (Revelation 2:18–29).

Reflection: Thyatira was a small town with many trades, and participating in these trades required one to belong to a guild. The guilds were wholly pagan, and at each official meeting, guild members were expected to pay homage to pagan gods who "blessed" the trade, as well as to participate in licentious activity as a sexual form of worship.

Because of King Ahab's wife and her notoriety throughout Israel's history, no person in his or her right mind in the early Church would have named a daughter "Jezebel," and no pagan parent was likely to have chosen to give a daughter a Jewish name with such abhorrent ties to someone else's religious history. From this we know "Jezebel" is a symbol, as are many other names in Revelation. "Jezebel" may or may not have been a female, and in fact, it could have even been a group of people, as feminine references in both Greek and Hebrew can be used to denote a multitude. Again, the false teacher(s) in this letter is guilty of the same grievances as the followers of "Balaam" or the Nicolaitanes in the former letters. Between this, the pagan worship taking place all over this area in relation to trade guilds, and this "Jezebel's" association with the name of the Old Testament character (who led Ahab and Israel astray toward the demonic worship of Baal), scholars believe the Christians of Thyatira were allowing some degree of idol worship to be a part of their new faith. The picture painted in this letter seems to be that a person or group was running around the church telling Christians that it was still okay to participate in the idolatrous system of guild meetings, possibly in an attempt to convince them that the adultery and sexual immorality were merely means to economic prosperity and were not a matter of the heart, over which Christ was truly Lord. Obviously, on so many accounts, such a "teaching" would associate one to a "Jezebel spirit."

Not all of the people of Thyatira were guilty in this, and it is to those whom Christ offers the gifts of ruling (literally "shepherding" in the Greek; verse 27) all nations with a rod of iron (protecting their people and defeating their enemies). He also mentions the "morning star," which indicates Himself in light of the coming triumph in the end of the book (Revelation 22:16). Together, these gifts state that the believer who holds onto the Truth of the Gospel and follows Jesus to the end will participate with Him in His Millennial Reign.

To Sardis, from the One who has the sevenfold (fullness of) Spirit of God and the seven stars: I know your works, and I know that even though you have a reputation as people who are alive, you are really dead. You better watch out and wake up. Strengthen that which remains, because even what little remains is ready to die. You don't live up to the requirements of God; you must go back to what you heard and believed in the beginning, and hold to it firmly. Repent and turn back to Me. If you don't wake up and become watchful, I will come to you, like a thief, suddenly and at an hour you do not expect. There are so few of you in Sardis who haven't defiled their garments, and it is to them that I say: You will walk with Me in white, because you are worthy. For all who are victorious will be dressed in pure white. Their names will never be blotted out from the Book of Life, and I will tell the Father and the angels that they are Mine. Anyone who has ears to hear must use their hearing to listen to, and understand, the Spirit's message to all the churches (Revelation 3:1–6).

Reflection: Sardis was known for two things: massive wealth and overconfidence. Before New Testament times, Sardis was the capital of Croesus, one of the wealthiest kings in the ancient world, with a nearly impenetrable defense system at the bottom of the steep hill the city sat upon. It was captured by the Persian King Cyrus circa 549 BC, and again by Antiochus circa 218 BC, and each time, it was because the opulent and brash city didn't feel it needed to set up a guard at night, making it easy for the enemy troops to invade and conquer the sleeping inhabitants.[41]

Their reputation of the citizens of Sardis was of a people very "alive," as Christ said, but inside, they were dead and lazy, believing (probably through the power of their money) that they had it all figured out. Christianity is inherently about focusing joyfully on the life after this one while the body is dying (2 Corinthians 6:9). The Sardinians had it in reverse.

In verse 2 of His letter, Jesus says they must be watchful. This appears as "Wake up!" in some translations. It's no doubt that, between both historic battles that went down like they did, they were used to letting the enemy slip under their noses unaware. Christ is here telling them that this symptom applies to them spiritually as well.

This church was not suffering from persecution like the others; that's easier to understand if there wasn't a "Christian problem" in this city: Believers in Sardis were scarce, and the ones who did live there weren't as passionate about Jesus as they once were.

We are reminded of lyrics from the song "Asleep in the Light" by Keith Green—one of the most anointed Christian songwriters in history:

> The world is sleeping in the dark
> That the Church just can't fight 'cause it's asleep in the light.
> How can you be so dead, when you've been so well fed?
> Jesus rose from the grave, and *you*!
> You can't even get out of bed![42]

Sardis was spiritually lethargic, immersed in maintaining a low profile while Christians were put to death all around them. Pagans kept bowing to the gods of wood, silver, and gold; they whistled and strolled, going about their daily lives as usual. But those few who were faithful would be draped in robes of purity and cleansed; their names would never be erased from the Book of Life.

To Philadelphia, from the One who is true, holy, and holds the key of David, who has the power to open what no man can close and close what no man can open: I know all of your works, and I have opened up a doorway for you that nobody can close. Your strength is small, but your faith led you to obey My Word, and you have not denied My Name. Behold! Those who say they are Jews, but who really make up the synagogue of Satan, will be made to acknowledge that I love you. You have been faithful to persevere, and I will protect you from the hour of temptation that is about to come upon the world. I *am* coming soon, so make sure that you keep holding to what you have so no man can take your crown. To those who are victorious, they will be pillars in the Temple of God, and their rightful place there will never be disturbed. The Name of God—and the name of His Holy City, the New Jerusalem, which will originate from heaven—will be written on them. I will also write upon them My new name. Anyone who has ears to hear must use their hearing to listen to, and understand, the Spirit's message to all the churches (Revelation 3:7–13).

Reflection: This letter bears striking resemblance to the one addressed to Smyrna. Not only were both without any complaints against the believers, they also mentioned that believers were being persecuted by those who made up the "synagogue of Satan" (which we've already addressed). The believers of these two congregations would receive a crown at the end of their earthly faithfulness.

The "keys" in this letter are not the ones to death and the grave like before, but of "David." This is a reference to Isaiah 22:22: "And the key of the house of David will I lay upon his shoulder; So he shall open, and none shall shut; And he shall shut, and none shall open." Christ has the ultimate power over all things related to salvation. Once He opens a door for a believer to be saved, no other person on earth has the power to close it. Putting the pieces together, scholars rebuild the picture thus: Christians were probably being excluded from worship by the Jews in Philadelphia, but Christ was allowing them to enter the spiritual and invisible synagogue or "Temple," of which they will be "pillars" (strong and immovable structures).

In Deuteronomy 4:34, the plagues of Egypt were called the "temptations of Egypt." The "hour of temptation" the faithful Philadelphians will be protected from is the coming, worldwide season of plagues and affliction for unbelievers known as the seven-year Tribulation.[43] (As noted prior, this is a major argument in favor of a pretribulational Rapture.)

Receiving any kind of "new name" was familiar to the Philadelphians, as their city had recently been renamed twice (once as Neocaesarea, and again as Flavia). Here, the "new name" is derived from Isaiah 62:2 and 65:15: "And the Gentiles shall see thy righteousness, And all kings thy glory: And thou shalt be called by a new name, Which the mouth of the Lord shall name." "And ye shall leave your name for a curse unto my chosen: For the Lord God shall slay thee, And call his servants by another name." Isaiah 56:5 also refers to "an everlasting name, that shall not be cut off." These verses, along with the letter's mention of the "Temple" and the "New Jerusalem," makes it clear that something major is coming that will completely redefine (rename) the believers in their future roles in the Kingdom of Christ described in Ezekiel 40–48. This will be consummated in the Millennial Reign.

To Laodicea, from the One who is the Amen, the faithful Witness, the start of God's new creation: I know everything you do, and I am aware that you are neither hot nor cold. I wish that you would be one or the other, but since you are lukewarm, I will spit you from My mouth. You think you are rich and don't need a thing. You think you've got everything you want. But you don't realize you're truly wretched, miserable, poor, blind, and naked. So here is My advice: Buy your gold from Me, which is gold that has been purified through the fire. Only *then* will you truly be rich! By your garments from Me so you are not wandering naked and ashamed. Buy your eye medicine from Me so you will be able to really see. I correct and discipline those whom I love, so be diligent in turning away from your indifference and apathy. Behold! I am standing at the door, and I am knocking. If you hear My voice and open the door to Me, I will come in and we can break bread together as friends. To those who are victorious, they will sit with Me on my throne, just as I was victorious and joined My Father on His throne. Anyone who has ears to hear must use their hearing to listen to, and understand, the Spirit's message to all the churches (Revelation 3:14–22).

Reflection: The letter to the Laodiceans is, in our humble opinion, one of the most misunderstood passages of this book. It is therefore quite a happy coincidence (or perhaps divinely arranged?) that it is the last of the seven churches we'll reflect upon before moving into the remainder of Revelation. Discussing how the letter is commonly viewed today versus its real context leads perfectly into the rest of the text. As we discuss the Laodiceans' financial situation and comforts, consider the comparison of this church's status to that of the Western world.

Here's what a lot of folks don't know that directly contributes to the meaning of the letter: The city of Laodicea was industrious and successful; its residents were made rich by several trades. One was the textile trade from black sheep (producing jet-black garments). The city also had a medical school noted for its success in ophthalmology (vision). Because of that, people came from all over the region to purchase an "eyesalve" (eye medicine scholars believe was made from powdered Phrygian stone) for countless vision and eye-irritation treatment. Laodicea was located near a spring that produced piping hot water. This water flowed from its origin in Hierapolis, past Laodicea, and farther to the south to Denizli. A little farther out on the map was Colossae, which had a natural cold-water spring, but the Laodiceans received their central water supply from the aqueduct between Hierapolis and Denizli, so it arrived lukewarm.

References in this letter to all three of these things (water temperature, eye medicine, and garments) have been drastically misunderstood. Let's consider the water first.

Many preachers stand at pulpits today interpreting the "lukewarm" warning to be something akin to: "God either wants you to be on fire for Him, or He wants you to man up and admit that you secretly reject Him. But it's time to stop riding the fence! Be hot, or be cold, but if you simply go to Church and don't really love Him, you are 'lukewarm,' and He will spew you from His mouth!" Such interpretations are convicting, but they miss the point. The Laodiceans personally had experienced receiving their water lukewarm. Both in antiquity as well as in modernity, beverages have been served hot or cold, but (not intentionally) lukewarm (and if they did—such as making "hot" cocoa cooler for a child, or what have you—it would be an exception, not a rule). Both hot and cold extremes have had many uses: Hot water cleanses, purifies, offers therapeutic elements for the body, etc.; cold water refreshes and revives, stimulates, cools the body, and so on. Lukewarm water has always been, and is today, useless for many reasons that we would seek water to treat. There are many contemporary opinions about what lukewarm water is like, but in the ancient world, it was particularly gross... People of earlier times didn't have the medicines we have today to combat illness, and lukewarm water has always been a bacterial breeding ground (germs don't survive as well in either temperature extremes). So, the water the Laodiceans received would have been more than a matter of mere taste; it would have endangered whoever consumed it, if it were not somehow purified. See, to the residents of "Lukewarm Water City," the letter wasn't about having an honest zeal for Jesus. If it was, then why would Jesus *ever* prefer them to be cold, as He said (3:15)?

Really allow yourself to think about that for a moment... Jesus stated—with no liberty in the Greek—that they *either* be hot or cold, but not somewhere in between. If a believers are still "on the fence" about Jesus, then they are closer to Him than if they reject Him entirely. They would still be closer to the possibility of salvation than if they rejected Christ completely, and if God is "not willing that any might perish" (2 Peter 3:9), then "lukewarm" is better than "cold," and it's not rocket science to come to such an obvious conclusion. The Holy Spirit can work with "somewhere in between," and we know that He would want to, since there is still room to "warm up" to God in regard to one's salvation. There is no doubt that God is loving and offers forgiveness, so wouldn't a loving God appreciate that the Laodiceans weren't completely cold? Wouldn't He encourage them to continue in their pursuit of spiritual growth, knowing they had the potential to become who He called them to be? One might argue that a syncretistic, idolatrous relationship with Jesus alongside other gods would fit the bill here (and scholars *do* believe idolatry was a problem for some of these folks), but wishing them to be "cold" in that case would still be like Christ saying, "Hurry up and reject me so you can fully love your gods." Is that possible? Technically, it could be, as we know God will eventually leave an idolater alone (Hosea 4:17). Some academics conclude this is the spirit behind the statement. But we believe that the stress of Christ's statement of *preference* ("I would thou be") renders this impossible. No matter what the circumstances, why would Jesus prefer someone with a cold spiritual condition over one that is still brewing? For Him to harshly rebuke the Laodiceans for idolatry and demand repentance is one thing; to tell them He would prefer for them to reject Him and damn themselves for all eternity is another thing entirely. It just doesn't align with what we know of Him to say elsewhere. It simply cannot make sense theologically considering the whole Bible's message of love and growth of those who are navigating their journey toward the invisible Kingdom amidst a sea of gods.

The answer, once the context of the Laodicean water supply is taken into account, is easy to find. Jesus wanted the Laodicean Gospel to be meaningful to the world around them, but if their Good News message was lukewarm, it was "without use." *Worse*, it was "dangerous": The message of Laodicea to the surrounding world was a nauseating, hazardous "bacterial breeding ground"!

What would bacteria in bad water affect?

The body of a human.

What would a bacterial Gospel affect?

The Body of Christ.

Jesus' words to the Laodiceans were that their outward witness to the world around them was nauseating, and worse than spiritually worthless, because they were willingly blind and spiritually filled with bacteria. Why? Because of *what* (rather than *who*) they placed their faith in—worldly wealth: "Because thou sayest, I am rich, and increased with goods, and have need of nothing" (3:17).

Some aspects of humanity never change. Each time serious trouble befalls mankind (as only one example, the September 11, 2001, destruction of the twin towers of the World Trade Center), people who otherwise would never attend a church flood religious centers and surround spiritual shepherds (church leaders) with the need for "higher" answers. A sudden dependency upon the Lord for answers and provision develops that no money can provide. Prior to that point, though, people are generally "comfortable enough to forget about God" as long as their mouths are fed and their pillow cushions are properly fluffed. The residents of Laodicea had everything they needed, assuming no person or tragedy upset their way of life, because they believed earthly financial status made them "rich" and "in need of nothing" while Jesus knew they were actually "wretched, and miserable, and poor, and blind, and naked" (3:17). A complacency had replaced their need for a Savior, and the Savior knew their hearts. What they claimed to be was a "hot or cold" use to the world, while their spiritual integrity was "lukewarm." Christ's response to this was to offer a list of what they needed on the *inside* in order to be truly repaired.

It was a short list: gold, garments, and eye medicine.

First, "gold" cannot be "bought," as it was the means of purchase in the first place (in the standard sense). We are reminded of Isaiah 55:1, which talks of buying "without money and without price." Therefore, the mention of "gold" here speaks of glory, brilliance, and magnificence as a metaphor (as noted in the "Common Symbols" section). Gold, as well as other precious metals, were not simply mined in perfect condition, but were drawn from the ores of the earth and refined in a fire, removing dross (random junk in the natural metals) and imperfections. The Laodiceans must "buy" their gold from Christ, trading their worldly comforts and riches for a kind of wealth only He can provide from a heavenly origin—that which is "tried in the fire" (Revelation 3:18): Their faith would need to be "tried" if they were ever to appreciate its value. Then, it would be worth far more than what perishes on earth: "That the trial of your faith, being much more precious than of gold that perisheth, though it be tried with fire, might be found unto praise and honour and glory at the appearing of Jesus Christ" (1 Peter 1:7).

Second, the "white" garment of purity in Christ (representing cleanliness and wisdom) removes "shame" and "nakedness" (Revelation 3:18), which the lucrative black-sheep textile trade of Laodicea cannot offer. To Sardis, the "dead" church, Christ said: "He that overcometh, the same shall be clothed in white raiment" (3:5a). So, in a similar vein, there is an "overcoming" and a "trying" necessary for the Laodiceans so far.

Third, the eye medicine (or "eyesalve" in the KJV; 3:18), if obtained through Christ, would remove their blindness. As noted, the medical school of Laodicea (specializing in ophthalmology) was where many in the ancient world would travel for help with eye problems. Laodiceans had at least human reason to believe they would be self-sufficient with issues related to vision, which "pops" Christ's words to them about "blindness" into new focus (no pun intended). But the loss of sight that He was referring to was, of course, spiritual.

With all the comforts they had on a daily basis, their faith was in need of testing to see if it was genuine. God doesn't just go around taking away the wealth or security of His followers, but when their wealth and security *replace* Him—that is, when their blessings are not used in a manner that accomplishes what God stands for—He has been known to allow certain trials. The exiles are, by themselves, an example of this (though they are not by any means the only time of testing of God's people, as both Testaments show).

Hopefully by now, you have a better understanding of what was going on in Laodicea that could have led Jesus to send (through John) such a letter…but we have said *all of this* to build to the climax of the whole word-picture Jesus provided: He stands at the door and knocks (3:20).

Once again, we arrive at a heavily misunderstood verse.

In most church services today, this verse is frequently used as a sort of altar call: "Jesus is standing at the door of your heart, knocking. Won't you let Him in? Won't you make the decision that today is the day you will receive Him in so He can fellowship with you and change your life for the better?" It's an invitation offered by well-meaning Christians to help others make a personal decision about faith in Christ. The invitation is typically followed by offering to lead the responder/respondent through the "sinner's prayer," bringing in a harvest of souls.

Please hear us: *We are not attempting to say that such a harvest is in any way unbiblical or that it does not fit the collective teaching of the Word, because it does.* Thousands of verses in both Old and New Testaments make the united statement that God loves all people and wants to transform sinners into the beautiful creations God intended them to be. We are not offended by such an altar call.

However, that's not the focus of this particular verse. This modern application doesn't capture the fullness of the image the Bible presents. Remember, this book is not an Epistle. Revelation is alternatively known as the Apocalypse; its content is eschatological and therefore must be kept in its proper context.

Consider what's being clearly—and literally—communicated here: A real congregation that existed in Asia Minor is being warned that Christ is knocking on the door of *His own house*, asking to be let into the *church* so He can break bread as friends with His followers. In such a scenario, the focus is not upon the heart of an individual believer saying a specific prayer at the time of conversion (though such an act is precious and well supported by Scriptures elsewhere). To the Laodiceans, in particular, as well as to all believers at this point in the book of Revelation that are in the same dismal spiritual state of health, and therefore to us, today, who likewise rely on worldly comforts in the last days when Christ can come "like a thief," at any moment...the emphasis of this verse becomes this: *Jesus is no longer in the building.*

This ancient "church of Jesus" therefore makes a powerful point in the verses following the letters to the seven churches: During the end times, there will be places dedicated to the worship of Jesus that miss the mark entirely; the "believers" within such places will find themselves void of their spiritual inheritance. Antichrist will—as the following pages of study show—inaugurate a one-world religion that looks like Christianity but is, in every way, fraudulent when it comes to what Christ stood for. When that happens, the presence of Jesus will be elsewhere, outside the assembling of those who call themselves believers.

Today, as He was then, Jesus is standing outside many churches, knocking. He wants to enter and "sup" (break bread) with the people who say they are His. But today, as then, there are church bodies just like the one in Laodicea whose members follow wrongful teachings, practice idolatry, pursue money and careers, and participate in social gatherings that pretend to be spiritually "rich" but are truly wretched, poor, blind, and naked. A salvation invitation at altar calls could certainly correct this problem on an individual level, but the call in this letter is to the leaders of the collective Body to restore worship to its proper place while *we* seek after *Him*:

> If so many Scriptures instruct us that we are to "go to" or "come to" the Lord, then traditionally, *we* are the knockers asking for God's grace and intervention. *Bible Gateway* provides this intel: "These words have often been romanticized in popular religious art, in pictures of Jesus 'knocking at the heart's door.' What is wrong is that Jesus is standing outside the door, excluded from the banquet like the homeless stranger in Amos Wilder's poem. The poignant plea, though directed first to the church at Laodicea, is strategically placed near the end of the series of messages as Christ's last appeal *to any congregation that has shut him out.* The beautiful 'invitation' is at the same time a severe indictment of a church that is self-sufficient, complacent and only marginally Christian."[44]

To those who have an ear to hear: Behold, Laodicea. Behold, today's Church. Behold, today's ministers. If you are complacent, if you are apathetic, if you are lukewarm, if you use church grounds as a place of showmanship or social status or dropping verses or casually hobnobbing while you bask in the comforts of this mortal experience, then Christ is no longer in the building. It's no longer about Him. He's outside, knocking, asking to be invited back into His own home, and a ministry endeavor devoted to a Man who's not even present cannot be anointed by the Man who's standing outside.[45]

The real meaning of the verse is even more convicting than the one we've assigned to it in contemporary times. The Body of Christ, as a whole, needs to be paying very close attention to these letters. They would be from God even if they weren't "sent by Christ" because they are canonical. But unique to all other canonical "letters," these are being written by a Source who trumps even the apostles, whom the early Church found to be the supreme authority. We are in the end times now, and Jesus *is* coming back. So, as we move closer to the times of apocalyptic trials, these warnings from the Savior should be just as important to us as the rest of this book.

Elders and the Four Living Creatures (Revelation 4)

IN THE FIRST VERSE of Revelation chapter 4, we see a shift from a historical perspective to a future one: "After this I [John] looked, and, behold, a door was opened in heaven: and the first voice which I heard was as it were of a trumpet talking with me; which said, 'Come up hither, and I will shew thee *things which must be hereafter*'" (emphasis added). Note the similarity of the word picture here to all prior mention of Jesus "coming in the clouds" with a "trumpet blast." As commentators acknowledge, this is the moment when the scene switches from things seen on earth to the mysteries revealed in the heavenly realm regarding the ultimate plan of God. John the Revelator is asked to "come up hither" through "a door...opened in heaven," because Christ is about to reveal "things which must be hereafter." Thus, futurists believe this is the marking of the point at which we are no longer reflecting upon the things of John's day *or* ours, but of future events we all still have yet to face—i.e., we are now departing from the Church Age to the end of all things. Many scholars also note that John's being taken up into the clouds is a foreshadowing of the Rapture of all saints. As we continue, consider that this is the first of a phrase John repeats throughout Revelation to introduce a new vision: "After this…" (see: 7:1, 9; 15:5; 18:1; 19:1).

John writes that he was "immediately in the Spirit" upon hearing Jesus call him upward (4:2). He sees a throne occupied by One who glistened like gemstones, and around the throne was an emerald green aura that circled Him like a "rainbow" (the sign of God's Covenant; Genesis 9:16). (Note early on that this vision is remarkably similar to what Ezekiel saw as recorded in Ezekiel 1:26–28. Likewise, Revelation chapters 4–5 bear many images in common with Daniel 7.) Around this main throne are twenty-four others, and on each one is seated an elder wearing white robes with golden crowns (Revelation 4:1–4).

Debate regarding the identity of the twenty-four elders has produced some radically different views. Many scholars cling to the easiest conclusion: They're the twelve tribal patriarchs of Israel and the twelve apostles, uniting the central figures of the Old Testament with those of the New Testament. But some argue that the redeemed will not sit upon thrones until after God's final plans come to completion. That there is an exception to this rule in the case of the twenty-four elders here is supported by how they are described. Revelation elsewhere (2:10; 3:4–5, 18, 21; 6:11; 7:9, 14) reviews what the redeemed will receive (white robes, crowns) if they are among the "overcomers" mentioned in chapters 2–3. Two categories of "crowns" are given specific treatment in Revelation as well. The *stephanos* are the crowns of those who have become victorious over something, while the *diodemata* crowns (of verses such as 19:12) belong to kings. The *stephanos* worn by the twenty-four elders in 4:4 denote crowns of victory in a trial, and we therefore find good reason to assume that the natural interpretation—patriarchs and apostles—is the most likely identity of the elders. This conclusion is further supported by the apparent consummation of the righteous from both Testaments: a consecration visible through acknowledging the "heroes" of the Hall of Faith (Old Testament) joined in perfection with "us" (New Testament redeemed) in Hebrews 11:39–40. This image becomes yet sharper by the visual of the future dwelling place of the Bride of Christ in Revelation 21:12–14. While we respect that other interpretations are possible, we are choosing to continue under the teaching that the elders are the Old Testament's twelve patriarchs and the New Testament's twelve apostles.

From the throne comes thunder and lightning, and before the throne are seven lit torches, "which are the seven Spirits of God" (or the sevenfold Spirit of God). In front of the throne is a body of water, sparkling like glass or crystal (Revelation 4:5–6a). (A deep dig into the words "thunder" and "lightning" shows that this phenomenon might have actually been a "voice" that one can "see," manifested into flickering flames. For more information on this exciting possibility, and to see how the New Testament Pentecost was a nearly irrefutable fulfillment of a promise that began at Mt. Sinai at the delivery of the Law, see *The Messenger* by Tom Horn, pages 101–129.)

Four "beasts" (or "living creatures"), covered with eyes on their front and back, are standing around the throne. "And the first beast was like a lion, and the second beast like a calf, and the third beast had a face as a man, and the fourth beast was like a flying eagle"; they had six wings, also covered with eyes, and day and night they said, "Holy, holy, holy, Lord God Almighty, which was, and is, and is to come." Each time these beings worship, the twenty-four elders fall down and worship the One on the throne, esteeming His worthiness to receive glory, honor, and power, for He created all things that pleased Him (4:6b–11).

Just like the elders, these "four creatures" inspire many interpretational differences. First, it should be stated that Ezekiel also saw four living beings of a similar (but not identical) description in the first chapter of *his* prophetic revelation (Ezekiel 1:5–14; also see 10:12–15, 20–22, and Isaiah 6). Together, these two visions, along with notes about the covenantal sign of the rainbow around the One on the throne in both places, paint a collective picture of the glory of God being realized in one Judge (Christ). The lion, ox, man, and eagle can, therefore, be interpreted as elements of the nature of Jesus, as many scholars and theologians have done since just after the writing of Revelation. Jesus is: 1) the Lion of the tribe of Judah, as emphasized in the Gospel of Matthew through the image of Him as King of Israel; 2) the servant "animal" (ox) or the Suffering Servant, as emphasized in the Prophets and the Gospel of Mark; 3) the sinless Man, as emphasized in the Gospel of Luke; and 4) the Eagle (mightiest and swiftest of the birds making its home in lofty nests) who is quick to soar down from His heavenly home to earth offer salvation as emphasized in the God-Man images of the Gospel of John. Not everyone agrees this is the best interpretation, especially since there are variations between the scenes in this vision compared to those of Ezekiel. However, the "four living creatures" of this scene appear in one of the most enigmatic passages in the whole Bible, and it would take a considerable amount of time to parse out all the possibilities. Additionally, because the Beast is in close proximity within this book, many earlier commentaries simply go out of their way to correct the term "beasts" as being a descriptor of the creatures in some translations, simply making a brief statement that the "creatures" or "living beings" (or equivalent) are some kind of mysterious, celestial, and heavenly servants of God without addressing them at length. Because this "characteristics of Christ" view has been steadily held by highly respected scholars since just after the time of John, this is the one we have chosen to give most focus upon here. Another possibility, according to Kendall Easley's Revelation commentary, is that the cherubim atop the Ark of the Covenant—which were not fully described in the building pattern of Exodus 25:10–22—were "winged guardian figures...with features of several animals," and that these living creatures are the "heavenly reality" of the characters upon the Ark's Mercy Seat.[46]

The Seven Seals
(Revelation 5:1-8:5)

WITHOUT DOUBT, even among serious scholars, the Lamb that appears in Revelation 5 is Jesus, and the scroll with seven seals is one that nobody in the universe is able to open...except this Lamb.

John sees the seven-sealed scroll, with writing on the inside and out, in the right hand of the One on the throne. A strong angel with a loud voice shouts: "Who is worthy to open the book, and to loose the seals thereof?" Nobody above, on, or under the earth is worthy enough, so John weeps (Revelation 5:1–4).

It is often explained that John wept because he had been promised he would be shown what comes next (4:1), and now he is frustrated because he thinks in this moment he will *not* be shown the revelation. It is surprising how many scholars adopt this view. A number of questionable conclusions can be drawn from this interpretation. Does John actually doubt that Christ will come through on His promise to show him what comes next? Such a thought seems absurd, and it paints John as crying out of a selfish, perhaps even childish, motive.

A much more logical deduction comes from the fact that John, a man whose Gospel shows him to be highly trained in theology and the history of Israel, immediately recognizes the scroll as the very Kinsman-Redeemer contract symbol that it is proven to be in the coming verses. And if nobody in the universe can open it, then it's natural for to John shed tears over the idea that God's Kinsman-Redeemer plan for mankind as contained in the contract will never be fulfilled—thus, humanity is doomed for all time. (If you haven't yet read about the glorious parallel of this picture as we wrote in our study of Ruth—or if it has been some time since you reviewed that material—we suggest returning to that beautiful comparison now, as it is one of the most powerful moments in this entire work!)

While John is sobbing, one of the twenty-four elders says, "Weep not: behold, the Lion of the tribe of Judah, the Root of David, hath prevailed to open the book, and to loose the seven seals thereof." John looks up and sees a Lamb that appears as if it had been slaughtered. He is adorned with seven eyes (the fullness of knowledge and wisdom) and seven horns (fullness of all authority), which represent the seven-fold Spirit of God. The Lamb steps forward and takes the scroll from the One who sits on the throne, and the twenty-four elders and four living creatures fall down before the Lamb. Holding golden bowls of incense "full of odours, which are the prayers of saints" and harps, they sing a new song about the Lamb who was slain; whose blood was the ransom for the sins of humanity; and who causes every tribe and every nation to become a Kingdom of priests for God who will reign on the earth (5:4–10).

Yes! Our Kinsman Redeemer—our Boaz, our *Go'el*—has opened the scroll, just as foreshadowed in the tiny book of Ruth! Such an unbelievable moment in time is well worthy of praise, so it's not a surprise that praise is the very next thing to take place in John's vision.

John looks around again, hearing the voices of thousands and millions together—elders, creatures, and angels—singing a song acknowledging that the Lamb who was slaughtered is worthy of power, riches, wisdom, strength, honor, glory, and blessing. Another song rises up from "every creature which is in heaven, and on the earth, and under the earth, and such as are in the sea," recognizing that blessing, honor, glory, and power belong to both the One on the throne as well as the Lamb, forever. While the four living creatures shout "Amen!" the elders fall down and worship the Lamb (5:11–14).

As John watches, the Lamb breaks the first of the seven seals. One of the four living creatures summons John to come and look up, and when he does, he sees a white horse. Sitting atop the horse is a conqueror of many battles who wears a crown and carries a bow (6:1–2).

The identity of this horse-rider is of great debate among scholars. Some believe he is Jesus, the victorious Gospel message, or the Church. This is most immediately recognized by: 1) the horse's white color, which is used in Revelation to represent holiness and purity; 2) the fact that the crowned Christ is riding a white horse while defeating His enemies in 19:11–16; 3) Psalm 43:3–6, identified as a messianic prophecy in Hebrews 1:8, describes the King of kings taking down His enemies with arrows; 4) this first of four horses is not connected to one of the "woes" (addressed shortly), and is therefore unlike the next three horses that have been almost unanimously identified with evil. Others conclude that this rider is, like those who follow, also evil, and quite possibly Antichrist, himself. Support for this possibility can be seen in the following: 1) Antichrist will, in so many ways, look just like Jesus (before he later shows himself to be the deceiver), so the Christ-like imagery here applied to Antichrist is intentionally showing this strong, external resemblance (see this reality in Revelation 12–13; also see how dark forces imitate the light in 2 Corinthians 11:13–14); 2) just as this rider is "conquering" those he opposes, the Beast is elsewhere "conquering" or "overcoming" (same Greek word, *nikao*) the saints in the apocalyptic scenes (Revelation 11:7; 13:7); 3) Zechariah 1:8–15 and 6:1–8 depict the horses belonging to the "evil angels of the four pagan kingdoms"[47] in the book of Daniel (chapters 2 and 7), which link the nature of all four horses to this same prophetic fulfillment here in Revelation 6:1–8; 4) Mark 13:5–6, Matthew 24:4–5, and Luke 21:8 all describe that, right before the Second Coming, an outbreak of false christs and false prophets will appear upon the earth, claiming that they come in the Name of Jesus, and misleading multitudes (also see: 2 Thessalonians 2); 5) the first four trumpets, as well as the first four bowls, are often viewed as representing parallel judgments (but not always), and in a book like Revelation with so many symbolic patterns, it therefore stands to reason that the four horseman would be parallel also; 6) as Beale notes, the fourth horse wraps up the activities of the first three, and since the fourth is "death," then the first is also representative of something evil: the demon locusts who wage judgment in Revelation 9:7 are *also* crowned horsemen. [48]

After taking all possibilities into consideration, we believe the white rider is Antichrist, or at least some symbolic manifestation of his influential, wicked power. With that established, traditional pre-Trib Rapture timing places the great removal (Rapture) of the Church at the moment this man is revealed, which is right here in the narrative of John's visions. So for our pre-Trib readers, the terrifying events in the book of Revelation from this moment forward can be read with the understanding that the Church has been removed from the world.

In 2 Thessalonians 2:4, we read that Antichrist "exalteth himself above all that is called God, or that is worshipped; so that he as God sitteth in the temple of God, shewing himself that he is God." The verse means just what it sounds like, and from an absolute, extreme literal interpretation, Antichrist will claim to be God. As an imitator of Christ, most scholars acknowledge the likeliness that he will claim to be Christ, Himself. Back in 1 John 4:3, we read of the many "antichrists" that will be in the world (apart from the eschatological Beast figure) and how to recognize them: "And every spirit that confesseth not that Jesus Christ is come in the flesh is not of God: and this is that spirit of antichrist, whereof ye have heard that it should come; and even now already is it in the world." Though this verse referring to what is "already in the world" cannot be talking about the Beast of

Revelation who had not arrived yet ("there many antichrists," 1 John 2:18 states) it directly addresses the "spirit" of anyone who, tragically, would deserve that title. Therefore, it stands to reason that when Antichrist, the Beast, rises in the last days, he will do both: claim to be the long-awaited Messiah *and* deny that the Jesus of the four Gospels was the Son of God.

The preposition "anti" can mean two things in Greek: "opposed to" and "instead of," denoting a "substitution."[49] Matthew 24:5 states: "For many shall come in my name, saying, 'I am Christ'; and shall deceive many," and later in the same chapter, verse 24, "For there shall arise false Christs, and false prophets, and shall shew great signs and wonders; insomuch that, if it were possible, they shall deceive the very elect." The preposition in the name "Antichrist" ("anti") therefore fulfills both definitions—he will be "opposed to" the true Jesus of the Gospels and position himself as the substitution (a pseudo-Christ), deceiving many as the long-awaited Messiah...even to the point that "the very elect" will believe what he says about himself. Genesis 3:15 prophesied the coming of two "seeds," one of the woman (fulfilled in Jesus) and one of the serpent, now fulfilled here in this man, the literal son of Satan, who will reflect the powers of his evil father, the evil one spoken of in the "Lucifer" and "king of Babylon" ruminations of Isaiah 14. He will be unlike anyone the world has ever seen, and the folks alive on the earth in that day will say so outright (Revelation 13:4). The following list is only a small overview of the ways he will outperform the most impressive men in world history:

- Speaking presence (Revelation 13:5; Daniel 7:8, 20)
- Supreme political power (Revelation 17:12–13, 17; also see Daniel 9:27)
- Military command (Revelation 19:19)
- Earthly wealth and extravagance (Daniel 11:38)
- Economic policies and organizational skills (Revelation 18:3, 12–17, 22)

- Persuasive powers of self-aggrandizement (Daniel 11:36)
- Patient, successful oppression of God's people (Daniel 7:25)
- Extremely attractive (Daniel 7:20)

Lastly, scholars have looked at the various descriptions of Antichrist throughout Scripture and have debated his future identity geographically and racially as a means of providing the world with additional ways to recognize him when he arrives. If we can figure out where he comes from and what people he belongs to, he will be easier to spot in the coming days. As fascinating and well-meaning as these trails of thought are, the results are all over the place, and any specific identification in these matters can only be mere speculation. But if we openly admit to speculation (and not dogmatism) in the matter, there are a couple interesting tidbits from Scripture that may prove helpful later.[50]

First, the prophecies of Daniel (chapters 2, 7, 8; more specifically, 8:8–9, 21–23) and in Revelation (13:1; 17:3, 7, 12, 16) describe the geographical origin and eventual expansion of the "ten horns," which represent the area of the world from which the Beast arises. Once these areas are compared to the biblical texts and history, they point to the Western division of Alexander the Great's Roman conquests in today's Western Europe. The people who took down the Temple in Jerusalem in AD 70 are identified as "the people of the prince that shall come" (Daniel 9:26), further supporting the idea that Antichrist will come from within the Roman Empire (also see Daniel 7:7–8; Revelation 13:7).

Racially, our first clue lies in the fact that Antichrist will not "regard the God of his fathers" (Daniel 11:37). This language is strongly similar to the language throughout the Old Testament describing evil kings of Israel (especially in books 1 and 2 Kings), which suggests that Antichrist may be a Jew. Further support for this theory is that the tribe of Dan is missing from the tribes in Revelation 7:4–8, giving Antichrist an entire tribe of ethnic Jews to originate from without having his existence taint the sacred bloodlines of God's people. (The reason Dan is missing is explained in the upcoming pages.) John 5:43, featuring words from the mouth of Christ, also possibly points to Jewish ethnicity: "I [Christ] am come in my Father's name, and ye receive me not: if another shall come in his own name, him ye will receive." At first, it doesn't appear that the other person who comes "in his own name" can only be interpreted as Antichrist, but when we look at the rest of Revelation and see the trust that the Jews will initially place in the Man of Sin, the pieces fit: Jesus, in this passage, was referring to "false christs," as scholars unanimously acknowledge. The uber-false christ—meaning the very epitome of this sign—will be Antichrist, and the Jews *will* "receive" him, at least at first. Therefore, Christ's warning could be viewed as an indicator that Antichrist will hail from the same ethnic background (but not by any means the same bloodline) as did Jesus. However, while many scholars bounce back and forth on the issue, providing reasons for or against the concept of Jewish ethnicity, one major argument is often overlooked: Antichrist will be the supreme imitator of everything Christ was, so, if for no other reason, Antichrist could likely be a Jew simply because Jesus was.

One question on our end that no one appears to be addressing is this: What if Antichrist is from the tribe of Dan, appearing and speaking in every way Semitic, but he simply lies and says he's from the tribe of Judah (like Jesus was)? Though we won't mention any names, there have certainly been American politicians who have "fudged" their history a little (well, a lot, we think) to indicate they have a more impressive origin than they truly do. In that case, Antichrist could make every claim about himself that directly imitates the true Messiah of the Gospels without anyone being able to prove otherwise (and those who *do* attempt to prove otherwise, even if they have great evidence, will easily be written off as conspiracy theorists attempting nothing more than smear campaigns). In 2 Thessalonians 2:9–11, we read that Antichrist is the one "whose coming is after the working of

Satan with all power and signs and lying wonders, And with all deceivableness of unrighteousness in them that perish; because they received not the love of the truth, that they might be saved. And for this cause God shall send them strong delusion, that they should believe a lie." The last two words of this passage are misleading in English, because the original Greek included the definite article ("the"). Antichrist is not just *a* lie, he is *the* lie: deception personified. No matter what this evil person claims to be, we can assume there is some twisting of his identity and origins. Therefore, our theory that he is ethnically a Jew, but lies about which tribe and location he's from, is a valid possibility.

In any case, as stated, all theories about Antichrist's origins are conjecture, but as watchmen of the signs, we should be open-minded to considering that he is possibly a Jew, maybe from the tribe of Dan, and most likely born in the Western region of the Roman Empire.

Keep all of this in the back of your thoughts as you see how the rest of John's book plays out...

John then watches as the Lamb breaks the second seal and follows again the summons of one living creature to "look up." He sees a red horse (the horse of war) whose rider has a sword and all authority to rob the world of peace, and battling and bloodshed take place throughout the earth (Revelation 6:3–4). The Lamb breaks the third seal, and John sees a black horse (the horse of famine) whose rider carries a set of scales (an instrument for weighing grain that was, in antiquity, a symbol of famine [Leviticus 26:26; Ezekiel 4:9–10, 16]). One of the four living creatures says, "A measure of wheat for a penny, and three measures of barley for a penny; and see thou hurt not the oil and the wine" (Revelation 6:5–6). (These measurements in John's day were between "eight to sixteen times" the cost of wheat or barley anywhere in the Roman Empire.[51] Most scholars agree that the scarcity of wheat or barley amidst an "unhurt supply" of oil and wine suggests the daily food dependency of the poor will be in major shortage, while the luxuries of the rich will not yet be affected at this point.[52] Uniquely, the scholars behind the *Jamieson, Fausset, & Brown* commentary interpret this to mean that food will be scarce, while "the oil and wine were to be spared for the refreshment of the sufferers."[53]) The Lamb breaks the fourth seal, and John looks up to see a pale green horse (the horse of death), whose rider is named "Death." This rider has a companion named "Grave." Between the two of them, they are given authority over one-fourth of the earth "to kill with sword...hunger...death...the beasts of the earth" (6:7–8). (This concludes the four riders, whose judgments are likened to those sent by God in Ezekiel 14:21.)

The Lamb then breaks the fifth seal, and John sees the souls of the martyrs who died for the Name of Jesus under the altar. They shout out to the Lord, "How long, O Lord, holy and true, dost thou not judge and avenge our blood on them that dwell on the earth?" Each is then given a white robe, and they are instructed to rest just a while longer until the remaining martyrs, their brothers and sisters in the faith, have joined them (Revelation 6:9–11). The Lamb then breaks the sixth seal, and a great earthquake ensues. The sun darkens to black, and the moon turns as red as blood (6:12). (This language is reflected in the prophecy of Joel 2:31.) The stars fall to the earth like figs shaken from their tree by a mighty gust of wind, the heavens roll up like a scroll, and the mountains and islands are all moved from their original places (Revelation 6:13–14). (The note about the heavens "rolling up like a scroll" is reminiscent of Isaiah 34:4.) Then everyone—"the kings of the earth, and the great men, and the rich men, and the chief captains, and the mighty men, and every bondman, and every free man" (seven people groups)—took to hiding in caves and between mountain rocks, crying out so that they might be crushed and buried by avalanches to escape the judgment of the Lamb, for the great day of wrath has come, "and who shall be able to stand?" they ask (Revelation 6:15–17).

As for the seven different categories of people who would hide, John uses numerical symbolism again to show completeness: *All* of God's enemies, from the greatest to the least, will seek to hide from

God, but they know He is inescapable, so they seek the relief of a quick death rather than face Him. This echoes the words of God's prophet in regard to this sixth-seal earthquake: "Enter into the rock, and hide thee in the dust, for fear of the Lord, and for the glory of his majesty...And they shall go into the holes of the rocks, and into the caves of the earth, for fear of the Lord, and for the glory of his majesty, when he ariseth to shake terribly the earth" (Isaiah 2:10, 19). The dust and debris loosened by the earthquake may be the cause of the sun blackening and the moon turning to blood as well.

Then John sees four angels standing at the four corners of the earth, holding back the four winds, and another angel appears from the east, carrying the seal of God. He shouts to the other angels, "Hurt not the earth, neither the sea, nor the trees, till we have sealed the servants of our God in their foreheads." John listens to those who are listed as receiving the mark of God—twelve hundred from each of the twelve tribes, totaling one hundred forty-four thousand (Revelation 7:1–8).

After this, John sees an enormous crowd made up of every nation, tribe, people, and language, standing before the throne and the Lamb. All of them are clothed in a white robe and hold palm branches in their hands. They are shouting, "Salvation to our God which sitteth upon the throne, and unto the Lamb." The angels are standing around the throne, the elders, and the four living creatures. In one accord, they fall before the throne and worship God, singing: "Amen: Blessing, and glory, and wisdom, and thanksgiving, and honour, and power, and might, be unto our God for ever and ever. Amen" (7:9–12). One of the twenty-four elders asks John who the white-robed ones are and where they come from. John answers, "Sir, thou knowest," and the elder says that these are those who died during the Great Tribulation, having washed their garments in the blood of the Lamb, which made them white. This is why, the angel explains to John, they stand at the throne of God day and night, serving Him in His temple, and He shelters them. Never again will they hunger or thirst, and they will not be scorched by the sun, for the Lamb of God will be their

Shepherd. He will lead them to the springs of the waters of life, and God will wipe away every one of their tears (7:13–17).

There are a number of things that need to be tackled here. First, as the number four is a Revelation symbol of the earth, John is not describing the shape of the earth as a flat square with an angel at each "corner"; rather, in context of the "four winds," this is a symbol of the whole planet and the cardinal winds (north, east, south, west), as well as a reflection of such images as the "four winds of heaven" from one of the apocalyptic prophecies (Zechariah 6:5). In the Bible, wind is noted to be a natural force of destruction (Jeremiah 4:11–12; 49:36; 51:1–2). Some scholars acknowledge that the direction from which the other angel approaches is a reference to where light "originates" (in this "earth" context, that would be the sun, which rises in the east). Other sources of blessing are related to the east, such as the location of the Garden of Eden (Genesis 2:8), the origin of the glory that entered the Temple (Ezekiel 43:2), and the magi who sought the Christ child (Matthew 2:1–2).[54]

The mark of God is obviously not to be confused with the mark of the Beast. Collectively, scholars believe the purpose of the mark of God upon the foreheads of the one hundred forty-four thousand is to gift these men and women with the supernatural ability to persevere during the coming Tribulation; whether that is a physical or spiritual provision, the answers vary. (Some believe the mark of God is given to strengthen them to endure what horrific events were just listed in chapter 6 regarding the first six seals. However, that is not the interpretation of the premillennialist.) God's "marking" system is similar here to that described in Ezekiel 9 (an angel marks true believers, protecting them from the Babylonians) and Exodus 12 (God's people mark their homes with the blood of the sacrificial lambs on the night of the first Passover). Generally, scholars also allow the one hundred forty-four thousand to be figurative language, as twelve is another "number of God" (twelve apostles, twelve tribes of Israel, twelve hundred from each tribe times twelve tribes as the number of the mark of God, and so on), while many futurists believe the number to be literal. Since this is the case, and interpretations around the rest of the book also vary, there is not a single idea everyone subscribes to as to whether this is a large group or a small one, in relation to the population of the earth in that day.

The one hundred forty-four thousand come into a parenthetic enlargement (they are further described) in Revelation 14:1–15:4. However, since they first appear here, we will address their identity at this point, and not later: Interpretations about just who these people are can be vast, including viewpoints such as: 1) the same people who were viewed as the multitude John saw in Revelation 7:9; 2) the *only* ones who will ever inherit the Kingdom of God (primarily a confusion from a false doctrine belonging to Jehovah's Witnesses); 3) Christians who have kept the Sabbath holy; 4) all the redeemed who died during the Church Age; 5) ethnic Israelites; 6) recently converted messianic Jews; 7) folks who have already gone to heaven who are being sent back for another mission; 8) those who will rule alongside Christ in the Millennial Reign; 9) the physical Jews who rule during the Millennial Reign while the Christians rule spiritually; 10) those who died in the first three and a half years of the Tribulation; 11) the Old Testament saints who died before Christ's First Advent; 12) those destined for martyrdom who are protected until *after* they have given their witness about Christ; and likely a billion others. Upon further study, many fall flat because of verses that refute them or because there are no verses that directly teach these concepts as being true.

For many who believe Christians will go through the seven-year Tribulation, the one hundred forty-four thousand are frequently viewed as symbolic of all of God's people in the Church Age. An extension of this postmillennial teaching often states that these marked ones will be paramount to the restoration of Israel during the Millennial Reign, which will include some or all aspects of the reinstatement of Mosaic Law. Though this method of interpretation has a great following, and we respect this as a valid opinion, this is not our conclusion.

Some discount the idea that Scripture is referring to the tribes of Israel in Revelation 7 as an ethnic race—those who receive the mark of God because they're direct descendants of one of the sons of Jacob—believing them instead to be a "spiritual Israel" (the Church universal), as supported by Romans 9–11. This passage states that: 1) not all of the descendants of Abraham will inherit God's promise to Abraham, as it is a matter of the heart, not birthright (Romans 9:6–9); 2) a large number of Israelites did not believe, and therefore, have rejected God (9:27– 33); and 3) Gentiles have been conjoined through the Branch (Jesus) of God's elect (11:11–24). However, Revelation 7 in no way suggests that these people receive God's mark *only* because they're related by blood to Jacob. The salvation or protection for those who receive the mark of God are obviously among the men and women who choose to follow Him. Therefore, as it pertains to the condition of the soul, *bloodline inheritance* is irrelevant...but we think there is reason to believe bloodline is key to *identity*.

As to whether or not they will be literal Jews, the plain, literal writing of Revelation 7:5–8 appears to suggest they are. The word "tribes" in the Bible always refers to ethnic Israelites, though here, in Revelation, it's not the same as the original twelve, providing another clue that a literal, ethnic identification is intended (for if a "spiritual Israel" was in view, the original names of the tribes would have sufficed). In Genesis 35:23–26, the tribes are as follows (and in this order): Reuben, Simeon, Levi, Judah, Issachar, Zebulun, Joseph, Benjamin, Dan, Naphtali, Gad, and Asher. In Revelation 7:5–8, there is no mention of Dan, and Manasseh is added. The short version of the backstory on this is that Jacob pronounced a blessing on Joseph's sons, Ephraim and Manasseh (Genesis 48:11–20), making them heirs among the tribes, technically bringing the number to fourteen total tribes. In Deuteronomy 10:9, it is stated that the tribe of Levi would not receive an inheritance, because this tribe made up the priesthood God promised to personally provide for, initially taking them off the list (thirteen). But, because Christ fulfilled their function forever (Hebrews 7–10), and this section of Revelation is not referring to that kind of inheritance, Levi is listed among those marked by God (taking the number back to fourteen). When Rachel's handmaiden gave birth to Dan, she considered it a judgment from God against her well before Dan ever had a chance to sin (Genesis 30:6). Then, in Judges 18:30–31, Dan was the first tribe that embraced pagan idolatry (they were essentially obliterated because of this), and in 1 Kings 12–15, after the split of Israel into two kingdoms, Jeroboam established centers of pagan worship in the lands of Dan and Bethel (which was on Ephraim's soil). Both Dan and Ephraim spiritually "prostituted" themselves, "divorcing" their "Husband" and forsaking their inheritance, and in Hosea 4:17, we see that God's response to such a decision is to leave them to their idols (also see Hosea 5:9, which states that Ephraim will be "desolate" in "the day of rebuke"). Once the idolatrous Dan and Ephraim are removed, we're back at twelve tribes—eleven original, Manasseh added in place of Dan and Ephraim never listed—who will be marked by God in Revelation. (It's interesting that Irenaeus believed the Antichrist would rise from the tribe of Dan![55]) If this section of Revelation is *only* about a "spiritual Church" and has nothing to do with Jewish ethnicity, the tweaks needed to arrive at the adjusted twelve are completely unnecessary, since they're all symbolic anyway.

We also believe the phrasing of Revelation 7 places the great multitude from verse 7 as an *addition to* the twelve tribes in the first half of the chapter ("every people" does not suggest Jews only), so they are seen separately. If that is the case, then the one hundred forty-four thousand could, in fact, be ethnic Jews (whether literal or figurative, numerically). Assuming for a moment that they are, using the same passage as those who seek to disprove this theory, the book of Romans refers to an Old Testament group called the "remnant" (as a couple of examples where we find this word, see Micah 5:7; 7:18; Haggai 1:12, 14; and Isaiah 11:16): "And so all Israel shall be saved: as it is written, 'There shall come out of Zion the Deliverer, and shall turn away ungodliness from Jacob'" (Romans 11:26). But note:

"All Israel" is a recurring expression in Jewish literature, where it need not mean "every Jew without a single exception," but "Israel as a whole." Thus "all Israel has a portion in the age to come," says the Mishnah tractate *Sanhedrin* (10.1), and proceeds immediately to name certain Israelites who have no portion therein.[56]

It seems most fitting to allow the natural reading of Revelation 7:5–8. Thus, we conclude that the people who receive the mark of God on their foreheads are Jews, and more specifically, the "remnant" Jews who are saved in that day through faith in Christ, the true Messiah. Due to the number twelve meaning "completion," we could say that "one hundred forty-four thousand" is symbolic for "all Israel." In other words, if we pretend that "twelve" is the equivalent of "completion," the math would be: completion *times* completion *equals* "the fullness of all," regardless of what that literal number would be. Bearing in mind the exception just noted in the source we quoted, the new equation is "the fullness of all who are saved through Christ."

The *purpose* of this group, we believe, will be to stand as witnesses, Jewish missionaries, from the time of their conversion to the time of their physical death, where they will join up with the Messiah they have now accepted. This is supported by the idea that immediately after the numbering of them in Revelation 7:5–8, a great multitude comes forth wearing white robes and holding palm leaves. (Some scholars have worked out the chronology of Revelation and believe that the one hundred forty-four thousand are saved as a direct result of the two witnesses in chapter 11, which we find to be quite possible. In fact, some believe this so heartily that they say this conclusion is "doubtless."[57] If this is true, then it naturally bleeds into the idea that this "complete" army of now-messianic Jews could be the reason Israel recognizes the Man of Sin for who he is and turns against him, either causing him to break his own peace treaty with them, or his broken vow is the final straw that tips the scales of their recognition of his true identity. Either way, we believe those two events to be close in proximity.)

With that in mind, consider that Paul is a kind of representative of the Jews (as suggested by 1 Corinthians 15:8). If his example is any indicator of the zeal and passion these messianic Jews will have in those days, we *may* be looking at one hundred forty-four thousand—*at least*—mini-Pauls running around in the last days. After the Epistles, we've seen how incredible that one man was in establishing the glorious Church of Jesus, right? So many discussions about Revelation refer to the end of the world, doom, gloom, and tragedy, destruction of the planet, and all kinds of sorrow. In the midst of this, however, God's plan paves the way for a massive multitude of Pauls to absolutely and irrefutably bombard the forces of evil with an end-time harvest larger than even the Christian growth described in the book of Acts!

God is so good. He is so, *so* merciful to the people He has created! That even while the world is raising up the anti-God-man, the Beast from the sea of humanity, and enthroning him above the true Son, God would personally provide a means to *still*—despite everything people have done against Him—come to redemption in the Name of the real Messiah…that's unfathomable! Pauls *everywhere*!

Oh my gosh, we could scream with excitement at this picture!

Folks, Revelation is not all bad news. If even a fraction of these messianic Jews follow in the footsteps of Paul, though the churches they "plant" in that time will be underground, we're talking about a New-Testament-style era of Christian passion the globe will have never seen.

Imagine: There they will be, in the future, when all hell literally breaks loose on the earth, damned and without hope, lost in the snares of the serpent's seed, feeling the demoralizing, internal weight of a religious faith built upon the promiscuous seduction of the whore of Babylon (false religion, addressed soon). Whatever technology in operation at that time—television, the Internet, electronic devices, etc.—will assail their every moment with news of what Antichrist is up to. Pictures of him shaking hands with foreign politicians will cover public walls, transportation hives, universities, apostate church buildings, and any other place the imagination can devise. If we're correct in our theology of the image of God, then these end-time sinners, too, will be made in that image and have just the smallest inkling in their discerning spirits that something isn't right about this ten-coalition leader. Something about his eyes are darker than they should be; something about that smile creeps them out and makes the hair on their arms stand erect; his foreign policies and worship demands look a little too close to what that old book called "Rev-something" that was written by a guy on an island somewhere that predicted this "superman" to be a grand deceiver; their great Gramma So-and-So said some revealing things about a "Man of Sin" that make him just look too similar to this "world savior"… They will watch his speeches, delivered against the backdrop of his intensely good looks and unparalleled articulation, and will believe that everything he says makes sense, drawing them back into his plan. He will outshine every human mega-hero who has ever lived, and the sheer volume of his world-dominating power will attest to every word that falls out of his mouth, reinstating the faith of the masses…but *something* is going to feel "off" about him that *some* of them can't ever completely shake. The invisible but vile smoke of hell swirling about his presence as he speaks with the tongues of demons challenges his authority for those with "eyes to see" in the latter days. Many will silence that internal voice, as is clear in the Word, but some will not, as is obvious by the ministry of this army bearing the mark of God. So, as they watch the destruction of the world crumbling around them and feel just the beginning seed of doubt in their beloved Antichrist, in walks—wait for it…

One hundred and forty-four thousand Pauls, marked with apostolic boldness by God, Himself, carrying the only message that saves, anointed by the Holy Spirit, preaching in the streets with a craving for holiness and love so unmatched that they will be willing to die mid-sermon, just like our disciple-making, God-fearing, kick-the-devil-where-it-hurts apostle!

WHOA! BOOM! Behold the power of God in the face of the grandest manifestation of satanic forces in the history of the world. Total knock-out. TKO! Game, set, match…then Jesus!

BOY that's powerful!

Hallelujah! Glory to the Prince of Peace! We can't *not* get excited about the light that outshines the darkness of this future time when God takes hold of it! An entire world will one day fall under the influence of Satan's son, but when the darkness is at its most permeating depths, a light will break through the suffocating stronghold, that solid rock of iniquity—not just cracking through, but busting it into smithereens and bringing a revelation of the Son of Glory to those who have not yet completely rejected Him.

Thank You, Jesus, for Your endless grace to the wicked human race…

As to the identity of the great multitude, Revelation 7:14 directly identifies these as the ones who have washed their garments in the blood of the Lamb and who have been saved out of the Great Tribulation. This seems to indicate that they are different from all who found Jesus prior to the start of the Tribulation. They also appear to be a different group from the tribes, because the tribes were numbered, and this particular multitude is one that "no man could number" (7:9). These "Tribulation saints" have been somewhat of a puzzle for premillennialists, leading to the question: "If the saints are raptured *before* the Tribulation, and therefore there are no believers on the earth during this time—and if the one hundred forty-four thousand are Jews—then who is this group, and how did they come to be saved? Furthermore, if they missed the Rapture, how can they join up with Christ? They missed their chance, didn't they?"

First, let us state quite firmly that we (along with the majority of scholars) believe the whole *purpose* of the Tribulation is to gather up the last of those who will come to the knowledge of God and be spared His wrath. (The scroll with the seven seals is God's plan of redemption, so the unfolding of it at the onset of the Tribulation is the unfolding of God's redemptive plan for all who have not yet received the Messiah as personal Savior.) Therefore, we have no problem believing this group is absolutely saved, as the Bible says here. Though some theological threads claim there will be no second chances after the Rapture, that makes no sense in light of Revelation 20:4, which talks of those who are beheaded because they believe. Again, if there were no second chances, what is the point of persecuting believers?

Second, though we don't know specifics yet, we also believe God will take up the saints, but will leave their ministries on earth in a way that they can continue the harvest even after we're gone. These ministries include platforms such as books, blogs, articles, online video sermons, or the Bible, itself (though one of Howell's popular theories is that Antichrist will have those largely destroyed and replaced with what he will teach is "the *real* Bible," cut and twisted from our current canon into a new, blasphemous, mangled, web-of-deception canon, and the true Holy Bible will be preserved only under the radar, in secret). Further, when the Rapture occurs, the teaching of the saints will live on in the memories of those who remain, and when a countless number of Christians are suddenly gone, they will take seriously what they had been taught, along with those who claimed to be Christians but didn't really believe in Christ until the disappearance of the rest of their congregations. All of this is in addition to those who come to Christ as a direct result of the one hundred forty-four thousand messianic Jews, as well as the "two witnesses" (we will address these men later, in our look at Revelation 11:1–13).

So, the idea that they can somehow come to know Christ is a nonissue for us.

As to their identity, most evidence (we believe) points to the idea that, because of the severe persecution on earth in those days against Christians, anyone who becomes saved *after* the Rapture is likely a

martyr. Most simply put, these "Tribulation saints" could synony-
mously be called "Tribulation martyrs" (not to be confused with those
martyred in the Church Age prior to the Rapture in 6:9–11).

Attending to their "joining" with Christ, the angel explains to
John that they are already standing at the throne of God day and
night, serving Him in His temple (7:13–17). Though they miss the
Rapture, we see clearly they are in the presence of God after death,
though their admission into His presence came at a much higher cost
than those who were able to escape God's wrath: "And I saw the souls
of them that were beheaded for the witness of Jesus, and for the word
of God, and which had not worshipped the beast, neither his image,
neither had received his mark upon their foreheads, or in their hands;
and they lived and reigned with Christ a thousand years" (Revelation
20:4b).

Before we move on, we will share a few brief notes regarding
the timing of all these events: Many premillennial scholars associate
the opening of the first six seals to be the beginning of the seven-
year Tribulation, while chapter 7 (the mark of God on the foreheads
of the one hundred forty-four thousand) is at the midway point
(approximately three and a half years in). If this is the correct understanding, then the seventh seal is in the early part of the second half
of the Tribulation. This places a number of events that we haven't
yet covered (the opening of the scroll, the death and resurrection of
Antichrist, the death of the two witnesses, the abomination of desolation in the Temple, and other occurrences) all between the first
six seals and the forthcoming trumpets and bowl judgments. Other
possibilities are that the seven years begin in Revelation 12 (around
the time the dragon is ready to devour the child of the travailing
woman who is clothed with the sun); and still others say it begins in
Revelation 16 (bowl judgments). While the authors of this book don't
claim to have all the answers—again, we subscribe primarily as pan-
Tribbers (it will all pan out in the end, so we should not allow this
discussion to cause division in the Body, or as Dr. Thomas Horn says,

"We should be ready for pre-Trib or pre-wrath alternatives regarding Rapture timing")—our personal approach to the book of Revelation is mainstream premillennial. (Some of our timing is around the idea that Revelation 9:3–4 shows that the seal of God protects the one hundred forty-four thousand from the fifth trumpet; this is material we will look at soon.) We will continue in our study as if that is the case, but we want our readers to know that they can fully expect our timing to be different than other works on this topic, and we respect those opinions also.

Finally, the Lamb opens the seventh and final seal of the scroll. As this transpires, there is a silence throughout heaven for about a half hour. John sees seven angels stand before God, who are each given a trumpet. Another angel approaches carrying a gold incense burner. He mixes a great amount of incense together with the prayers of God's people and offers it upon the altar. After the angel pours this mixture out, the smoke ascends to God, and the angel fills the incense burner with fire from the altar and throws it down to the earth. Thunder and lightning ensue, and there is a terrible earthquake (Revelation 8:1–5).

Utter silence in heaven, Bible interpreters say, is possibly in respect for the prayers of God's people, but it could also be the awesome reverence for God's forthcoming judgment upon the planet and a moment of silence for what the people on earth are about to experience.

The source of the thunder, lightning, and earthquake here appear to be, at least in part, the prayers of the saints, including the early martyrs who were killed innocently, merely because they believed in Jesus. Revelation 6:10 says the martyrs "cried with a loud voice, saying, 'How long, O Lord, holy and true, dost thou not judge and avenge our blood on them that dwell on the earth?'" This moment—this absolutely terrifying moment at the beginning of the end of the world—is their answer.

The Seven Trumpets
(Revelation 8:6-11:19)

Earlier, in the section called "Judgments: Parallel or Sequential?" we discussed the possibility that the later bowl series of judgments could possibly be a recapitulation of the trumpets told from different perspectives, like the popular "three blind men and an elephant" example. As a reminder: Though we do acknowledge this to be a possibility, it is not our personal belief, due to the evidence we listed in support of a sequential approach. We therefore proceed in the order John the Revelator gave, treating the trumpet sequence of judgments alone and separate from the later bowls.

Following the earthquake, John watches as the first angel blows his trumpet of judgment. Hail and fire, mixed with blood, are thrown down from heaven, setting ablaze one-third of the earth, one-third of the trees, and all of the green grass (8:6–7).

The mention of "blood" here could be either symbolic or literal, though the symbolism throughout Revelation argues for the possibility that it may be a *color* intended, rather than a particular substance: Hail and fire could certainly be explained naturally through some

kind of extreme weather, or an electrical or meteorological phenomenon, so it stands to reason that the "blood" could be as well. The most
popular theories include the prospects of a polluted, discolored rain,
volcanic activity, literal bloodshed caused by those on the ground who
are struck by the falling objects or lightning, or simply the overall
color of the sky (but see the next two trumpets, handled together). If
taken literally (and we believe it can be), theories abound as to where
this blood would have come from, but seeing as this is the hand of
God at work, mere conjecture as to the origin of blood (which is all
anyone can offer on this) is unnecessary. As one-third of all trees are
burned up, the sources of food on the planet are also affected, as well
as the earth's capability of producing oxygen through photosynthesis
(which depends on foliage).

The second angel blows his trumpet, and a great "mountain" on
fire (scholars sometimes believe this to be a volcano) plunges into the
sea, turning one-third of the water into blood, killing one-third of all
sea life, and destroying one-third of all ships on the water's surface. The
third angel follows with his trumpet blast, and a burning star (possibly an angel) called "Wormwood" (sometimes called "Bitterness")
falls into rivers and springs, causing one-third of the water to become
"bitter" (poisonous), and many people die from drinking it (8:8–11).

Trumpets two and three effectively wipe out a third of both
kinds of water on the earth: the "sea" (saltwater) and the lakes/riv-
ers (freshwater). These authors worked together on a full-length book
specifically related to an incoming asteroid "Apophis," thus named by
NASA, which has been dated to arrive on (or near) the earth in 2029.
If it is pulled from its course by the earth's gravitational energy, then
the impact could be catastrophic, fulfilling precisely what is described
by John here. In this book, *The Wormwood Prophecy* (available at
SkyWatchTVStore.com), we surveyed possibilities of both the second
and third trumpets and compared them to the "water into blood" phenomenon in Exodus, as well as the natural procession of events that
would follow. We highly recommend the *Wormwood* book for a more

complete treatment on what may be happening here. For now, suffice it to say that the plagues of Egypt were, in addition to ancient Egypt, experienced in a small town in the 1980s, on Lake Nyos: Iron-rich water from the deepest crevices of the lake floor was released via earthquakes (called a "limnic eruption" or "lake overturning"), then mixed with the rest of the water, forming iron hydroxide (basically rust) and turning the color of the entire lake from blue to a deep red. If you've ever bitten your tongue and tasted that iron/metallic taste of blood, or smelled blood and equated it with that "wet metal" smell, then you can probably see how the Israelites/Egyptians may have described a high-iron, gas-poisoned, blood-colored water substance as "blood," *if* that was what they were dealing with. It wouldn't be much different than other passages of the Bible in which something scientific (such as Earth orbiting around the sun) is described in words that the writers found familiar (such as the "rising" and "setting" of the sun in Psalm 113:3). Though vast bodies of "blood" are a hard thing to imagine scientifically, interpretations of Revelation do allow for figurative language to describe God's hand behind natural disasters. Likewise, poisoned waters could be a result of astrological-object contact, as we observed as recently as 2007 in Carancas, Peru. A seven-to-twelve-ton chunk of chondrite space rock, traveling at twenty-seven thousand miles per hour and heated to three thousand degrees Fahrenheit, hit the empty plains. Local villagers were struck with extreme illness, the symptoms of which were so wide and seemingly disconnected that it initially looked hopeless that they would isolate a cause or come up with a cure. This particular space rock was only the size of "a dinette set,"[58] so its poisoning potential that would threaten local water supplies is obviously incomparable to any sizable trumpet judgment that enters large bodies of water or moving streams. Nevertheless, within only hours of collision, a mysterious sickness had spread to the point that the nearby residents began to whisper that the meteorite's scattered debris was, among other theories, "cursed."[59] We can only imagine the damage of a colossal impact such as that described in Revelation.

The fourth angel blows his trumpet, and one-third of the sun, the moon, and the stars are stricken, darkening one-third of both the day and the night (Revelation 8:12). (A natural reading explains that, quite simply, one third of the planet's sources of light are put out by this event.) John hears an eagle flying through heaven, "saying with a loud voice, 'Woe, woe, woe, to the inhabiters of the earth by reason of the other voices of the trumpet of the three angels, which are yet to sound!'" (8:13).

The word "eagle" here could be translated to "vulture." Both are birds of prey, linked in Matthew 24:28 as harbingers of tragedy. As Morris notes, the warning of the eagle to the inhabitants of the world points to one central thing: "There is a deepening of intensity" on the forthcoming judgments.[60]

The fifth trumpet is blown, and John sees another star (or angel) fall to the earth. This star is given the key to the bottomless pit (or abyss), and when he opens it, smoke billows out from within, like an enormous furnace, turning the sunlight and air dark. Hordes of locusts with the power to sting like scorpions erupt out of the smoke, looking like horses in battle, but with human faces and some kind of golden crown atop long, womanly hair and featuring sharp teeth like those of lions. Their armor is made of iron, and the sound of their wings makes such a noise that it is like a throng of chariots racing into battle. They are not allowed to sting those with the mark of God on their foreheads, but they're given freedom to torture everyone else for five months under the decree of their king, the angel from the bottomless pit whose name is Abaddon (Hebrew) or Apollyon (Greek). In the days of the scorpion-locusts, people will seek death but will be unable to find it. They will long for the release from agony death can bring, but it will run from them. This first terror is now past, but behold! Two more terrors are coming (9:1–12).

Wow... There is a *lot* of frightening imagery here.

To begin, since the angel is here depicted as a personified star, it is not completely accurate to say it is a "fallen angel," as some interpreters do. Rather, this "star" is "descending downward"; it's not "fallen" in a spiritual sense. Be that as it may, an evil angel is here identified by many, in part because he is given the power to unlock the abyss (but note that he was "given" that "key," which Beale says may point to the idea that this is a servant of Christ who "holds the keys" to death and the grave[61] [1:18; also see verse 20:1]).

Let us make a quick side note here before continuing... Some skeptics of biblical literature find the language around locations of the afterlife to be off-putting, because they are not viewed as being scientifically possible. This is true not only for Revelation, but for the terminology used throughout the Word and in Hebrew history since time immemorial. Such terms as "Sheol," "Hades," "Gehenna," and even "hell," which are all depicted as being at the center of the earth (Matthew 12:40; Ephesians 4:9; Psalm 63:9; Amos 9:2; Isaiah 14:9, 15; Ezekiel 31:16–17; 32:27; 2 Peter 2:4) causes many problems. But Revelation scholar Kendall Easley profoundly captures how we feel with his statement, "It is best for us to think of this as their 'theological geography of the universe' rather than as their 'scientific geography.'"[62] (He goes on to point out the irony that even in today's scientifically enlightened world, people write "up in heaven" and other such figures of speech all the time and nobody ever thinks a thing of it. It's only when the Bible uses similar phrasing that people get riled...) With that in mind, rigidly developed arguments for or against these locations being literal is a job for a book with a completely different purpose than this one. Simply put: We believe these word pictures are helpful to understand what it was John saw, and for now, it doesn't need to be more than that.

With that said, the imagery of this "abyss" is mentioned elsewhere in Revelation (11:7; 17:8; 20:1–3) as the place where the Beast and the Dragon are contained, and upon studying it against concepts of the lake of fire (where those whose names are not written in the Book of Life will be cast; 20:10, 14–15), they are not the same place. Easley describes the visual of earlier "abyss" language as imagining a giant underground cavern with a small, narrow hole at the top that is kept shut and locked. Under this "door" is years' worth of horrible, choking smoke from a "sulfurous, crude-oil burning furnace"[63] packed in with no escape. When the door is unlatched, the smoke belches up from the ground and permeates the air, darkening everything. Easley's description is helpful, though scholars also rightly note that "the original readers would have conceived the Abyss to be in the depths of the sea."[64] This complicates the idea of escaping smoke and heat, which perhaps makes the concept of a "volcano rising from the sea" a better visual than an underground cavern.[65]

Whereas we are not insisting that the abyss must be interpreted to be a real place that forces Revelation's figurative language to present an absurdity, the judgments upon the earth—as guided by the sovereign hand of God and possibly involving the natural elements—are real (even while there is room for symbolism). Locusts in particular still plague the earth to this day, especially in the Middle East—and they, too, have a lifespan of five months—though albeit they don't look like those who will spring up at the sound of the fifth trumpet. Unlike natural locusts, these will be wholly demonic, causing such agony to those they torture that the victims will want to die, but they won't be able to. Honestly, the description of these creatures is so bizarre and so disturbing that very few sources have much to say about John's vision here. However, Easley visits the concepts of the symbols (thought to be figurative and nonliteral because of John's use of "like" or "as" in these verses) and suggests the following meanings (along with our own notes):

- **"Horses prepared for battle"**: Battle-ready horses are specifically bred and trained to be stronger and outlast a standard riding horse. Thus, the impression here is that John says these demons will show up well-prepared for what they are told to do.
- **"Crowns of gold"**: A symbol of authority and/or victory, suggesting the demons will be victorious in their mission to torture humanity.

- **"Human faces"**: Possibly inferring intelligence; humans are above the animal kingdom in this way, but a "human face" on a satanic bug might symbolize that they are capable of a higher level of reasoning.
- **"Women's hair"**: Many scholars, not just Easley, believe this refers to extreme antennae (but Easley reminds his readers that Parthian warriors of antiquity intentionally wore their hair as long as a women's because it was a sign of "fierceness").
- **"Lions' teeth"**: An obvious characteristic of a wild predator willing and able to devour its prey.
- **"Iron armor"**: Denotes militaristic preparedness (other scholars say this could be a radically pronounced and rippled thorax that is natural to locusts).
- **"Sounds of the wings like charging horses"**: With no biblical evidence to suggest how large these are, this could be a swarm, as of locusts, or it could indicate that the creatures are incredibly large on an individual basis.[66]

Interestingly, though "seeking after death" and "not being able to find it" was inconceivable in John's day, we are nearing a time now when that may not be difficult to imagine. Transhumanistic sciences are every day increasing toward the goal of achieving immortality. We are now capable of replacing more human body parts with machinery than ever before, and only a tiny, bureaucratic ribbon called "bioethics" is keeping us from altering our human DNA to take on the characteristics of animals that can outperform (and outlive) our finite bodies. When has it *ever* been true of the human race that a man who wanted to die couldn't do so by his own hand? Yet, the literal interpretation of this section of Revelation suggests that death will not even be possible. In fact, John states this twice! "And in those days shall men seek death, and shall not find it [1]; and shall desire to die, and death shall flee from them [2]" (9:6). Though any thread of concentration on this idea is mere conjecture to most Bible scholars, scientists not only think it's conceivable, but they're championing the idea, celebrating every little step we make toward the dream of our self-controlled immortality. At the very least, it's worth considering John's warning before we pass the point of no return in today's laboratories…

The sixth trumpet blasts, and from the four-horned altar in the presence of God, a voice tells the angel with the trumpet to release the four angels bound at the bottom of the Euphrates River. These angels—who are prepared for this very hour, day, month, and year—are released and proceed to kill one-third of the world's human population. John hears their army, which is comprised of two hundred million mounted troops. John also sees a vision of these horses and riders, writing that their armor is red like fire, as well as dark blue and yellow. The horses' heads are like lions, and from their mouths come billowing smoke, fire, and burning sulfur. One-third of all the earth's people are killed by the fire, smoke, and sulfur. Their power comes from their mouths and tails, which are like snakes and have the power to inflict injury. However, the people who do not die from this still refuse to turn to God and repent of their wickedness, murder, witchcraft, sexual perversion, and theft. They continue to worship their demons and the idols made of gold, silver, bronze, stone, and wood—idols that cannot see, hear, or even walk (Revelation 9:13–21).

As the number "four" represents the earth in Revelation and "horns" represent authority, the "four-horned" altar is believed to symbolize God's sovereignty to exact a worldwide effect of His trumpet judgment (also see Exodus 27:2).

Though some scholars believe these four angels are good, the vast majority of academics rightly see that there's no reason a good angel like this would be bound. There is an Old Testament prophecy mentioned many times regarding an army from just north of the Euphrates River that God will use to punish Israel (Isaiah 5:26–29; 7:20; 8:7–8; 14:29–31; Jeremiah 1:14–15; 4:6–13; 6:1, 22; 10:22; 13:20; 46:4, 6, 10, 22–23; Ezekiel 38:6, 15; 39:2; Joel 2:1–11, 20–25).[67] These four "angels" at the bottom of the Euphrates River could be associated with these prophecies. John's description of a vicious, evil army at this time would remind his early readers of the barbaric Parthians, who bordered the eastern boundary of the Roman Empire. However, no such army appears to be in mind as soon as the strange horses are described. Though the Parthians were known to twist the tails on their horses so they resembled snakes,[68] that's where the similarities end. It's clear that whatever John sees is principally satanic.

The worship of idols made of gold, silver, bronze, stone, and wood who cannot see, hear, or walk is a first-century word picture. However, such gods were not just empty decorations, as Paul made it clear they were objects of demon-worship (1 Corinthians 10:19–22) and therefore were crawling with the presence of real dark forces. When Antichrist comes to inaugurate the one-world religion, he may not have to be as obvious as to endorse idols of first-century influence in the homes of his followers in order to accomplish the same offense against God. That he would be brazen enough to insist on himself being the main object of worship is a no-brainer, and participating in such an act will, Revelation teaches, tragically lead to being visited and attacked by the very demons the people of earth will someday venerate…whether or not they realize *that* is what they are worshipping. Idolatry of any kind is a form of Satan worship.

Will Antichrist and his cronies someday build an idol that *will* appeal to the modern mind, above the archaic, static statues of old? We think that's not only feasible, it's a biblical promise (Daniel 9:27; 11:31; 12:11; Matthew 24:15–16; Mark 13:14; Revelation 13:14). Yet despite the massive number of crude graves in that day from the army led by fallen angels from the Euphrates, people will refuse to repent.

John then sees another mighty angel coming down from the heavens, surrounded by a cloud. A rainbow arches above his head, his face shines brightly like the sun, his feet are like pillars of fire, and in his hand is a small scroll that had been opened. As he stands on earth, his right foot is in the sea and his left is upon the land. He lets out a great shout, and the seven thunders answer him. John is about to write what he hears when the seven thunders speak, but another voice comes from heaven and tells him to keep the message of the seven thunders a secret (no scholar knows what is said, but as the narrative implies, that's intentional). The angel with one foot on land and one in the sea raises his right hand toward heaven and swears an oath in the Name of the One who lives forever, who created all the earth, the heavens, the sea, and everything that lives in those domains. His oath is that there will be no more delay, that God's mysterious plan will be brought to its final conclusion with the sounding of the seventh trumpet, just as the prophets had foretold (Revelation 10:1–7).

In the Old Testament, clouds, when they accompanied a traveler or group, symbolize the presence of God (Exodus 13:21; 40:34; 2 Chronicles 5:13–14), and the pillar of fire brings to mind the Israel's journey through the wilderness (Exodus 14:20). The rainbow is the sign of the Covenant (Genesis 9:8–17). This angel's face is shining like the sun, which, as stated earlier, signifies a majestic connection to God. Despite the similarities of the description of this angel to Christ earlier on, Christ, in Revelation, is not an "angel." One foot on land and one on sea not only portrays a being of massive size, it also symbolizes authority over both the earth and its waters. As far as seven thunders "answering," recall that "thunder" in the Bible is frequently synonymous with God's voice, and here, the number seven indicates the fullness of God. Whether this *voice* was God's own or not is uncertain (though some of our sources think so, like Bruce Barton stated firmly in his commentary),[69] though it's clear that it was from a heavenly servant at the very least.

This swearing of an oath by the angel regarding what God has told the "prophets" is a paramount moment. We see two worlds collide between the books of Revelation and Daniel (one of those very prophets) in this moment:

And I heard the man clothed in linen, which was upon the waters of the river, when he held up his right hand and his left hand unto heaven, and sware by him that liveth for ever that it shall be for *a time, times, and an half*, and when he shall have accomplished to scatter the power of the holy people, all these things shall be finished. (Daniel 12:7; emphasis added)

We will get to this "time, times, and an half" in a moment. For now, tuck it in the back of your thoughts and simply remember that the angel said God's mysterious plan is finally going to be completed. Also take note that "prophets" here does not just refer to those in the Old Testament, but to any prophet up to the writing of Revelation (therefore, New Testament prophets are included).

Then, the voice from heaven speaks again, instructing John to take the scroll from the angel standing on land and sea. John obeys, and the angel tells him to eat it, warning him that it will taste as sweet as honey, but it will turn his stomach sour. John eats the scroll as instructed, and it is sweet in his mouth, but makes his stomach sour. He is then told he must prophesy again "before many peoples, and nations, and tongues, and kings" (Revelation 10:8–11). (This is the commissioning of John as a prophet, modeled after a similar incident when Ezekiel was told to eat a scroll and obeyed, then was instructed immediately after tasting its honey sweetness to go and speak God's words to Israel [2:9–10; 3:1–4]. The "sweetness" is a symbol that God's Word is good, while, for John, the message of world destruction is stomach-turning.)

John is then given a measuring stick and told to go measure the Temple of God and count all those present who are worshipping. He is not, however, to measure the outer courtyards, as they have been given over to the nations, who will tread the holy city under their feet for forty-two months. Power will be granted to the two witnesses, and they will prophesy—while wearing burlap for those 1,260 days.

These two prophets are the two olive trees and lampstands that stand before the Lord. If any man hurts them, fire comes from their mouths and devours their enemies. They have the power to shut up the heavens so it will not rain while they prophesy, as well as the power to turn water into blood and to strike the earth with as many plagues as they want as often as they wish. When their testimonial work is done, the Beast (Antichrist) will come up from the bottomless pit and make war against them. They will die, and their bodies will lie in the streets of Jerusalem where Jesus was crucified—which is now spiritually Sodom (a symbol of moral depravity) and Egypt (a symbol of oppression and idolatry). For three and a half days, all people, tribes, nations, and folks of every language will see them and not be allowed to bury them. The work of the two witnesses will have so tormented the people that there will be joyful celebration and exchanging of gifts upon learning of the two men's deaths. But after three and a half days, the Spirit of God will breathe life into the witnesses, and they will stand up, striking terror into those who see them arise. A loud voice from heaven will call them to come up, and they will ascend to the clouds of heaven in the sight of their enemies. At that time, an earthquake will hit the city, destroying a tenth of it, and seven thousand people will perish, while everyone who remains gives glory to God out of terror. The second terror is past, but behold! A third is coming (Revelation 11:1–14).

Even the brightest scholars admit that Revelation chapter 11 is "extraordinarily difficult to interpret"[70] and has therefore led to an immense number of diverse interpretations. Because of this, we will allow the Bible to speak largely for itself, making only a few potentially helpful comments.

The "Temple of God" that John is sent to measure is—in context of the Holy City Jerusalem and the courtyards that have been given over to the nations—on the earth. This is a scene similar to the one in Ezekiel 40–42, when that prophet was also told to watch while another man measured the Temple and report to God's people what he had seen. However, since the Temple had been destroyed a number of years before the writing of Revelation, this could either be a reference to a future rebuilding of the Temple on earth or figurative language referring to: 1) the New Temple that will be in the New Jerusalem during the Millennial Reign; 2) a symbolic representative of the Church universal during the Church Age; or 3) a prophecy regarding the eventual salvation of the Jews (there are many other possibilities as well). The latter is what we tend to think is the truest interpretation because it fits within the context of Ezekiel 40–42, which, at that time, foreshadowed a restoration of the exiles. Romans 11:26 also foretells this kind of restoration, and Jesus mentioned this event in Luke 21:24: "And they shall fall by the edge of the sword, and shall be led away captive into all nations: and Jerusalem shall be trodden down of the Gentiles, until the times of the Gentiles be fulfilled."

The Temple in biblical times was in the center of three courts. The inner court was for priests; the next court outward was for ceremonially clean Jews to worship and segregated the men from the women; and the very outer court was where Gentiles could worship or learn more about the Jewish God. "Measuring" symbolized marking certain portions of the city to be either saved or destroyed (2 Samuel 8:2), and it can also imply God's authority and ownership of a section (2 Kings 21:13; Isaiah 34:11; Lamentations 2:8). In John's vision, the inner courts and Temple are saved, while the outer court and the rest of the holy city is vulnerable to disaster. The ones guilty of "trampling" here are Gentiles. Considering what Jesus said in Luke 21:24, this could be a prophecy regarding the salvation and rescue of the Jews (represented by the Temple and the Jews-only courts). However, because the prophecy spares only the Jews who are in the priestly or inner court, it doesn't spare those *outside* the holiest place, which means the real identity of those who will be kept from harm is the "remnant."

In Daniel 9:27, we learn that Antichrist enters a seven-year agreement with the Jews, and we believe that, for the first half of that time, the Jews will be allowed to worship in their Temple again. Now, remember Daniel mentioned "a time, times, and an half"? Scholars across all interpretational schools of thought understand this to be "a year, years, and a half-year," or, "a year, two years, and a half year," meaning three and a half years. That also could be broken down as "forty-two months" or "1,260 days," which is how long the "nations" will "trample" in John's vision of measuring the Temple and inner court. This vision takes place, then, in the *middle* of the seven-year Tribulation, when Antichrist breaks the covenant he had with the Jews and dishonors their arrangement, setting up the "abomination of desolation" as foretold in the Gospels, Daniel, and Revelation (Matthew 24:15–21; Daniel 7:25; 9:27; 11:31; 12:11; Revelation 13:14). The remnant will be spared!

The identity of the two witnesses is another hot-button topic in the scholarly universe. Because everyone is destined to experience the "first death" (mortality; see Hebrews 9:27)—and Enoch and Elijah did *not* die in that way—a lot of folks believe they will be the two witnesses. However, one major "first death" exception to the rule in Hebrews is the Rapture, which will take every true believer up into the clouds, making any of the raptured saints eligible to Enoch and Elijah levels of escaping the first death if that were the only qualification, so that interpretation may not hold. One possibility relies on taking into consideration Exodus 7–11, 1 Kings 17:1–7, and the power the two witnesses will be given to stop rain, turn water into blood, and send plagues in the Name of God (Revelation 11:6). This embodies the power of Moses and Elijah together. Moses and Elijah were also witnesses at the Transfiguration of Christ (Matthew 17:1–7). Recall also how prophecies can have multiple fulfillments. Malachi prophesied God would "send...Elijah the prophet before the coming of the great and dreadful day of the Lord" (Malachi 4:5). Earlier, in volume 2, we showed that, at the time of Christ, this was John the Baptist who came in "the spirit of" Elijah (refer back to that section if you wish, and recall that this is not a reincarnation teaching). If Malachi's prophecy also has a double fulfillment, the two witnesses *could be* Moses and Elijah.

Though views about the witnesses' identities are endless, the premillennialists largely believe them to be two literal, end-time people (not figurative symbols), although "burlap" (sometimes "sackcloth"), because of its association with the prophets of old, could simply signify some kind of outward appearance that identifies them as God's true witnesses in that day (for more information on the meaning of these clothes, also see Genesis 37:34; Revelation 6:12; 2 Samuel 3:31–32; 1 Kings 20:32; Matthew 11:21). Two witnesses in Zechariah's time were Joshua and Zerubbabel. The use of olive oil in lampstands during their story brought the power of the Holy Spirit to their ministry and message (Zechariah 4:1–6). Therefore, these two witnesses in Revelation "are the two olive trees and lampstands that stand before the Lord," or, two prophets powered by the Holy Spirit. Scholars, including those who follow premillennialist theology, do not agree whether these men will be carrying out their ministry in the first or second half of the seven years, and there are good arguments on both sides. They're either refuting Antichrist's popularity and warning of his coming betrayal midway in, or they're preaching after his betrayal to bring in the latter-Tribulation harvest.

Finally, the seventh trumpet is blown, and loud voices in heaven shout: "The kingdoms of this world are become the kingdoms of our Lord, and of his Christ; and he shall reign for ever and ever" (Revelation 11:15).

The timing initially seems odd here, as it is too soon for the Millennial Reign. Futurist-literal scholars believe this statement from the voices is a literary prolepsis or rhetorical anticipation—in this context, a prolepsis would be the recognition of the start of something that will be completed soon. Imagine you go see a tragic play. The opening narrative says, "Here lies Sarah. Sarah died defending her family." The storyline then "rewinds" to its beginning to explain what happened to Sarah. This is a prolepsis. In this heavenly moment, the voices are stating the completion of something that is only just beginning, before it "rewinds" to show details of the progressive fulfillment. However, the fact that it *has* begun points to an important fact: The powers of the earth, formerly belonging to Satan, have here transferred to Christ. This fact is seen in the following praise from the twenty-four elders who fall from their thrones to the ground and worship God:

> We give thee thanks, O Lord God Almighty, which art, and wast, and art to come; because thou hast taken to thee thy great power, and hast reigned [You have assumed Your power and have begun to use it for Your reign]. And the nations were angry, and thy wrath is come, and the time of the dead, that they should be judged, and that thou shouldest give reward unto thy servants the prophets [the time is now to judge the dead and reward Your prophets], and to the saints, and them that fear thy name, small and great [and *all* the holy saints]; and shouldest destroy them which destroy the earth (11:14–18).

Then, in heaven, the Temple of God is opened up, and the Ark of the Covenant can be seen from within it. Lightning, thunder, a hailstorm, and a terrible earthquake ensues (11:19).

The Woman and the Dragon (Revelation 12)

As is often the case with Revelation, the identity of the woman and her child in this next portion of Scripture has produced upwards of twenty different possibilities. The identity of the dragon, on the other hand, is essentially a slam-dunk, single answer across the board. We will continue in the same pattern we've been following thus far, looking first at what John saw, and then discussing the symbolism in his vision.

John writes that a great wonder appears in heaven (most folks imagine this to be the night sky, not the brightly lit place of worship that "heaven" can imply): A pregnant woman is clothed in the sun and a crown with twelve stars sits upon her head, while the moon is beneath her feet. She is in agony from birthing pangs, so she cries out in pain. Another great wonder appears: An enormous, red dragon emerges with ten horns. He has seven heads, and wears a crown upon each of them. With his tail, he sweeps away one-third of the stars and casts them to the earth. He then stands in front of the pregnant woman, waiting to devour her newborn as soon as it is delivered. The baby who is born from the woman is to rule all nations with an iron rod, and he is then caught up unto God and His throne. The woman flees to the wilderness, where God has prepared a safe place for her to stay for 1,260 days (Revelation 12:1–6).

Matrimonial language throughout the Old Testament that refers to God's people in "married woman" terms leads many interpreters to believe the woman represents Israel. In some places, "she" (Israel) is also viewed as pregnant (Isaiah 26:7; 66:7; Micah 4:10; 5:3). A countless number believe this starry mother is the Church. We personally agree that she represents Israel, as that matches the symbolism well, while we don't agree she is the Church universal (in part because the Church is supposed to be presented like a "virgin" in 2 Corinthians 11:2). In Joseph's dream, the twelve first sons of Jacob (the fathers of the tribes of Israel) were "stars" (Genesis 37:9), and this woman is wearing a crown with twelve stars. Furthermore, the very first—*ever*—messianic prophecy in Genesis 3:15 says in strikingly similar language: "And I will put enmity between thee [the devil or "serpent"] and the woman, and between thy seed and her seed; it shall bruise thy head, and thou shalt bruise his heel." Jesus said, "Nation will rise against nation, and kingdom against kingdom. There will be famines and earthquakes in various places. All these are the beginning of birth pains" (Matthew 24:7–8, NIV; cf. Mark 13:8). These "birth pains" Christ taught about were the signs of the end times, as illustrated in the very kinds of famine, earthquakes, etc., that have been occurring in Revelation up to this point.

When the woman has given birth, she flees from the dragon to a safe haven God has prepared for her. Recall that Antichrist breaks his promises to Israel halfway through his reign (three and a half years into the Tribulation), turning on her and setting up the "abomination of desolation" in the Temple. Just after his note about birth pains, Jesus also said, "When ye therefore shall see the abomination of desolation, spoken of by Daniel the prophet, stand in the holy place, (whoso readeth, let him understand:) Then let them which be in Judaea flee into the mountains" (Matthew 24:15–16). This is remarkable evidence in support of the idea that the woman is Israel (or "Judaea"), and that this moment when she flees from the dragon is an overview of a broken contract between Antichrist and the Jews at the midpoint of the Tribulation.

There's an incredibly popular theory that when the nation of Israel does follow Christ's advice to flee from Antichrist, they will hide in a rocky place in modern Jordan called Petra, which was called Sela in the Bible (meaning "rock"; Isaiah 16:1; 2 Kings 14:7). Today, Petra is uninhabited (though highly toured), but because many of the structures where people lived and worshipped are carved directly out of the side of mountainous rock, the ruins are still largely habitable. Daniel 11:41, says, "He [Antichrist] shall enter also into the glorious land, and many countries shall be overthrown: but these shall escape out of his hand, even Edom, and Moab, and the chief of the children of Ammon." Though we're not yet sure exactly why, Antichrist's power will not be able to penetrate these three countries. Petra's territory overlaps with the ancient city of Edom, and the only way to get there is to travel by horseback on a narrow access road called the Siq. The terrain is too rocky and restricting to invade with any grounded transportation, making it an ideal place to hide from enemies.

Psalm 2:7–9, in direct reference to the Son of God, says He will rule all nations with a "rod of iron." Jesus is the Son of God, surely, but He is also *a* son of Israel (from the tribe of Judah). Jesus, too, was "caught up" (Revelation 12:5) to God like the woman's baby in John's vision. Reading about His Ascension event shows that He went to the throne of the Father in every literal way (Acts 1:9–11). One day, as the prophets envisioned, He will rule all the nations in the Millennial Reign. The dragon waited to devour the woman's child, which scholars link to the event of Herod's slaughter of all baby boys in the attempt to wipe the Messiah out (Matthew 2:16).

Therefore, we share the opinion of many that the woman is Israel (not Mary, in particular, as some say), and the baby—or Baby, now that we've identified Him—is Jesus. As far as the dragon, that will become clear in the context of the next part of John's revelation; then we will briefly discuss the "stars" he "wiped out."

John then sees a war break out between the angels of God led by the archangel Michael on one side and the dragon and his angels (obviously evil or fallen angels) on the other. The dragon loses the battle and is forced out of heaven, he and his angels. This creature—"that old serpent, called the Devil, and Satan, which deceiveth the whole world"—is thrown to the earth (12:7–9).

In clear, unmistakable, self-interpreted terms, then, we can see that the "Dragon" is Satan. It's so clear that we don't even need to address conflicting theories (and they're not convincing, anyway).

The "stars" that he swept from the sky earlier on are believed to be angels as well. Dr. Michael Heiser notes that angels "are also called 'stars' (*kokebim*). Indeed, the very designation 'host' draws on descriptions of celestial bodies in the Old Testament (e.g., Gen 2:1; Jer 8:2)."[71] (Recall also that in this very book, in Revelation 1:16, the "stars" in Christ's hands are the "angels" of the churches.) As far as whether they are holy or wicked angels, that depends on the interpreter. Some are reminded of the wicked angels that left heaven as a result of Satan's influence, and because the angels in the former scene are cast down at the same time the Dragon's tail swiped across the heavens, this is a possibility: "And the angels which kept not their first estate, but left their own habitation, he hath reserved in everlasting chains under darkness unto the judgment of the great day" (Jude 6). There may be another explanation, though. We have yet to talk about Daniel's visions about beasts and horns, as it is most relevant in Revelation 13, but as our soon-coming explanation will show, Antichrist is the "boastful little horn." In Daniel 8:10, we read that this little horn "waxed great, even to the host of heaven; and it cast down some of the host and of the stars to the ground, and stamped upon them." Though scholars sometimes interpret these "stars" to be holy saints of God, this verse feels too close to the scene of the Dragon and the woman to disregard this link. As Antichrist is the Dragon's primary end-time servant, then it would still be through the Dragon's influence (symbolized by his tail) that these angels could have been knocked down. Since angels are spirits, we don't believe they could be injured in a bodily way like we can, which complicates things further. And, in the second of these two woman/Dragon scenes, a war breaks out between Satan and the angels of heaven, and he loses, without any mention of the death of—or even harm to—any of the celestial host. Therefore, Beale may be correct when he concludes that the angels the Dragon sweeps away "refers to persecution of God's people," because stars represent churches on the earth earlier in Revelation.[72] (Also note that Beale disagrees with the theory that the Dragon scene has anything to do with the fallen angels of Jude 6.)

John hears a loud voice from heaven acknowledging that the Kingdom of Christ has come at last, along with salvation, power, and authority, for the enemy who accuses the saints has been thrown down. The voice continues, proclaiming that the testimony of the blood of the Lamb given by those who were willing to die for His Name have defeated him; therefore, there is reason to rejoice, but the devil knows he has little time left, so he is angry, and terror will come upon the earth and its waters. John then writes that the Dragon pursues the woman who had given birth to the Child, but she is given the wings of an eagle to fly to her place of safety in the wilderness where she will live under protection for three and a half years. The Dragon attempts to send a flood to drown her from the waters of his mouth, but the earth assists her and swallows the water, so the angry Dragon declares war upon the rest of her children who keep God's commandments and share the testimony of Jesus (Revelation 12:10–17).

Satan's kingdom of evil is going down. When Israel flees, he is unable to catch up with the woman as she is given some kind of provision of swiftness (symbolized by wings). He tries again to kill her with a flood, which may or may not be literal water, as a "flood" is an Old Testament reference to devastating wickedness (Psalms 18:4; 32:6; 69:1–2; 124:2–5; Nahum 1:8), and the "sea" the Beast arises from is symbolized as wicked humanity, further suggesting that this particular "flood" may be a human army of Antichrist. However, she evades that attack as well (possibly with an earthquake). The "war" the Dragon declares against her and her "children" will not be successful, as the following chapters show.

As to the identity of the woman's other offspring, there is one question we can't answer with certainty. It's obvious that, if she is Israel, then her children would be Israelites. However, they are here depicted as not just Jews, but Jews who keep the testimony of Christ. That brings to mind the one hundred forty-four thousand with the mark of God, but it would not make sense that they are going into hiding. It's possible that some messianic Israelites will hide, while the marked ones don't, but it's also possible that those with the mark of God have already completed what they've been called to do by the time they are made to flee. Though we don't have the answer to this because these events have not happened yet, the overall picture is clear: God will protect His elect during the wars of the last days.

Beasts from Sea and Earth (Revelation 13)

As we finally reach the moment when the Beast, Antichrist, is officially in the picture, we see another beast as well—one who comes from the earth. Before we address these matters, however, we should look at the prophecies of Daniel. Because we already partially covered what Daniel saw back in the section on the prophets, this will be a quick review.

In Daniel 7–8, the prophet sees four "beasts" rising up from out of the sea. Revelation 17:15 interprets the symbol of the sea for us: "The waters…are peoples, and multitudes, and nations, and tongues." In other words, any rulers from this water arise by human systems—such as by inheritance (kings) and through elections (presidents). They're not heavenly leaders by God's appointment. Earlier in our study of the Major and Minor Prophets, we explained that the first beast was a lion with wings of an eagle who had its wings torn off, and it is afterward carried to land where it stands like a man, and it is given a man's mind. The second is a bear with three rib bones in its mouth who is told to "Arise, devour much flesh." The third is a leopard with four wings and four heads who is given "dominion." The fourth is the worst, "dreadful and terrible, and strong exceedingly," who has ten horns and teeth of iron.

As Daniel considers the horns of the worst (fourth) beast, a "little" horn—with "eyes like the eyes of man, and a mouth speaking great things"—grows outward and knocks out three other horns (7:8). (Because he is called "little," it has been suggested that he will have small beginnings—a no-name politician, perhaps, who doesn't initially appear very impressive or intimidating. Clearly, that is a short-term descriptor of who he will eventually come to be.) The Ancient of Days (God) is on His throne and defeats the beast, silencing the boastful words of the little horn (7:9–11). Then, Daniel sees Jesus:

> I saw in the night visions, and, behold, one like the Son of man came with the clouds of heaven, and came to the Ancient of days, and they brought him near before him. And there was given him dominion, and glory, and a kingdom, that all people, nations, and languages, should serve him: his dominion is an everlasting dominion, which shall not pass away, and his kingdom that which shall not be destroyed. (7:13–14)

An angel then interprets Daniel's vision about the beasts and horns, saying:

> The fourth beast shall be the fourth kingdom upon earth, which shall be diverse from all kingdoms, and shall devour the whole earth, and shall tread it down, and break it in pieces. And the ten horns out of this kingdom are ten kings that shall arise: and another shall rise after them; and he shall be diverse from the first, and he shall subdue three kings. And he shall speak great words against the most High, and shall wear out the saints of the most High, and think to change times and laws: and they shall be given into his hand until a time and times and the dividing of time [again, three and a half years]. (7:23–25)

In both visions of Daniel (the first being in chapter 2), God cuts off the power from the earthly kingdoms, ultimately to establish this one by the Son of Man. However, before that happens, the four beasts and ten horns (eleven, counting the boastful one with a mouth) will have their heyday on earth.

Though Daniel saw the beasts rising from the sea (of humanity), in Daniel 2:17, the angel says the beasts will come forth from the earth—again, rulers among men. Because of world history, the beasts are easy to interpret.

The national emblem throughout Babylon at the time was a lion with the wings of an eagle, and at times, this "lion" appeared with a man's face. Nebuchadnezzar was the king of Babylon, and he literally lived like a "beast of the field" (4:25) after he went insane, allowing his nails to grow like "birds' claws" and his hair to grow like "eagles' feathers" (4:33). Seven years later, his mind was restored (4:36) like the first beast who was given the mind of a man. Clearly, if the beasts are kingdoms, like the angel said, the first one is the Babylonian Empire.

The Medo-Persian Empire is the bear (second beast), who is on his side (7:5) as a symbol that one side of this empire was stronger (Persia), which was true. It is eating (or chewing on) three rib bones, just like Persia eventually consumed Babylon, Lydia, and Egypt, and the command it is given to devour flesh reflects its wide expansion to the north and west.

The third beast is a leopard, one of the swiftest creatures in the animal kingdom ("wings" are a symbol of extra speed), just as Greece was swift in its many conquests of much of the ancient world. Alexander the Great completed his conquests through four generals who moved *fast* on the ground (four wings). After the death of Alexander the Great, the empire divided into four "heads of state" leaders, explaining why this beast has four heads.

The fourth and final beast, also described as the most dreadful and most powerful of all, is the Roman Empire. Daniel doesn't describe this beast with as much detail, but he notes that it had "great iron teeth: it devoured and brake in pieces, and stamped the residue with the feet of it: and it was diverse from all the beasts that were before it," which describes the rise of the Roman Empire that crushed any who opposed it.

The ten horns on the fourth, the angel says, are kingdoms. Premillennial scholars almost unanimously agree that this ten-nation coalition will, in the end times, look like Rome all over again, because Antichrist (the "little horn") springs from the fourth beast (the Roman Empire). Ten kings (politicians) will unite with Antichrist's agenda and make war against God. Interestingly, the governments of Europe have already been agreeing to unite in this way, voluntarily eliminating their own autonomy and regional boundaries and signing over their authority to a unification organization called the European Economic Community, which claims "economic integration" as its top goal. This started back in March of 1957 when Belgium, France, Italy, Luxembourg, the Netherlands, and West Germany signed a treaty known as—*of all things!*—the "Treaty of Rome." (Seriously, what Daniel saw was precise down to the letter! And all of his "beast" visions were foreshadows of literal future events, arguing for a literal interpretation of the rest of his visions that come to completion in Revelation.) Though the Treaty of Rome got its name from the place where it was signed, the title alone is alarmingly prophetic. Not surprisingly, scholars believe this pattern will continue until there are ten powerful nations. Antichrist, the "little horn" very few people will see coming, will uproot three other "horns" (nations) and with his braggadocios mouth, establish himself as a world power...but not until *after* he has made a covenant with Israel (Daniel 9:24–27). (You may have noted that the beast of Daniel "uproots" three kingdoms, bringing the number to *seven*, while the Beast of Revelation still acknowledges *ten* full kingdoms in cooperation with Antichrist's reign. This has caused some debate, but it is not without an answer. Most agree the ten kings remain in Daniel but are subdued by Antichrist and absorbed into the first ten. So these three that are "uprooted" remain independent kingdoms, but in name only, as they are brought under authority of Antichrist's main ten kingdoms. Note that Russia has tried (at the writing of this work) to "absorb" the Ukraine in this way.

To bring closure to our look back at Daniel's prophecies, note the rock that was thrown seemingly out of nowhere to the nation-stack statue (that Daniel saw in the second chapter of his book) is the Kingdom of Christ. It will take down all nations and establish itself as the final authority forever. The mysterious fourth Figure that appeared in the furnace in the book of Daniel is a widely known Christophany—Jesus, Himself, was the one "like a son of the gods."

As a final consideration before we move on to the arrival of the Beast, 2 Thessalonians 2:3–8 refers to an end-times figure that "restraineth" or "withholdeth" Antichrist from being revealed before, or outside of, his appointed time. Although theories abound as to who or what this force could be, a look at the function of the Holy Spirit shows that He is the only One who has this kind of limitless power as it relates to the subject of sin (Genesis 6:3; John 16:8–11). Most scholars whose works we have read agree. These Scriptures from 2 Thessalonians collectively make the statement that the Restrainer (the Holy Spirit) moves out of the way (leaves the earth), allowing the prophetic events of Revelation to transpire. In other words, the reason we haven't already begun to see the fulfillment of Revelation is because the Holy Spirit has been preventing it. Therefore, since the Beast is here appearing in Revelation, the Holy Spirit and His restraining force that holds back the arrival and revealing of Antichrist has just left the earth in the narrative. (We know the Holy Spirit makes His current home in the hearts of believers, as a great volume of Scriptures in our Epistles studies have shown, but John 16:8–11 makes it clear that He is also present as a major convicting Presence upon the earth, and much of how He operates is *through* the people of God. His departure among the people of earth for the rise of Antichrist then argues for the timing of the Rapture to be *before* the introduction of Antichrist. Since Antichrist is a key character throughout the Tribulation, the

timing of the Rapture and the removal of the Restrainer is pretribulational, according to many scholars. Though this is the interpretation
that makes the most sense to us, we are not dogmatically insisting
this is the only possible way to follow eschatology. We are providing
one relevant argument in the mix that contributes to the chronology of Revelation's events. But one crucially important note must
be made about the Restrainer's departure: Without the Holy Spirit,
one cannot truly become saved [John 3:3, 5], so although He does
leave, He will still meet sincere seekers where they are and confirm
the testimony of Christ in the hearts of those who observe frightening events and wonder whether "this Jesus fellow of the Gospels" was
truly who He said He was. Revelation 11 shows the two witnesses'
success in converting the masses to Christianity, so even pretrib interpreters keep some presence of the Spirit in view up to the Tribulation's
halfway mark, or shortly thereafter. As shown in the coming pages,
an attitude shift takes place between the seals and trumpets and the
later bowls, wherein men stop repenting and only curse God; that is
the reaction on a global scale. This could indicate the entire ministry
of the Restrainer is completed by then, but even that interpretation
leaves out the entire nation that will believe in Jesus when He arrives
to establish the Millennial Reign [Isaiah 66:8; Zechariah 12:8–12].
Only God knows for certain, but these are the characteristics of the
ongoing debate. We personally believe that the "leaving" of the Spirit
from earth represents a dramatic increase of evil that God allows for
the purpose of consummating His ultimate end-times plan, not that
the Spirit would ever be "unavailable" to respond to a sincere soul,
ever, as that simply does not agree with His ministry as outlined in
the Word of God. With the Restrainer gone, Antichrist will finally
have the opportunity to arise and fool the world, but throughout the
Tribulation and into the Millennium, people are coming to believe in
Christ. So, although we believe the Bible to express that there will be a
seismic diminishing of the presence of the Spirit in the way He is oper-
ating *now*, we maintain that God would never appoint any human

soul on the earth to damnation if there was a chance of redemption, simply because God is "not willing that any should perish" [2 Peter 3:8–10].)

Now, onto Revelation chapter 13…

John sees a Beast (Antichrist) rising up from the sea with seven heads and ten horns, and each horn wears its own crown. On each of its heads is written a name that blasphemes God. The Beast looks like a leopard, but it has the feet of a bear and the mouth of a lion (a combination of the beasts from the vision of Daniel representing empires that historically opposed God's people with extreme political and military power). The Dragon hands his own power over to the Beast, along with his throne and authority. One of the heads on the Beast appears to be fatally wounded, but the wound is healed, and as soon as it is, the whole world stands amazed at the miracle and gives the Beast their total allegiance, worshipping the Dragon for having given the Beast such power. (Antichrist will recover from a fatal head wound as one of his many Christ-lookalike miracles and signs.) They also worship the Beast, believing that there is none greater than he, and no one can fight against him. The Beast is then allowed to speak blasphemy against God and do whatever else he wants for forty-two months—including disparaging God's Name and those in heaven—and decreeing war against God's people, conquering them, and ruling over every tribe, people, language, and nation. People all over the world whose names are not written in the Lamb's Book of Life worship the Beast (Revelation 13:1–8).

John switches gears for two verses and appeals directly to his reading audience: "If any man have an ear, let him hear. He that leadeth into captivity shall go into captivity: he that killeth with the sword must be killed with the sword. Here is the patience and the faith of the saints" (13:9–10).

Then John sees another beast (this is the false prophet; Revelation 16:13; 19:20; 20:10), this time coming from out of the earth. Just like a lamb, he has two horns (he appears Christlike on the outside, resembling the Lamb), but his voice sounds like a dragon (his words are satanic). He has all the same powers and authority as the first Beast, and he causes all people of the earth to worship the first Beast, whose fatal head wound has been healed. While everyone is watching, the beast from the earth does all sorts of miracles, including bringing fire down from the sky, and through these wonders, he is able to deceive the people of the world, ordering them to make an idol of the first Beast who had resurrected from his fatal wound. (The clear meaning here is that Antichrist will be resurrected from the dead, just like Jesus, but with Satan's power; the "wound" *could* also be something like a stroke that doesn't have an outward sign of injury.) The second beast then gives power to the idol so it can speak, and the idol decrees that anyone who refuses to worship it will die. He forces everyone—from the lesser to the greater of men, rich people and poor people, freemen and bondsmen—to receive a mark on their right hands or their foreheads. No one can buy or sell anything anywhere unless they have the mark of the Beast, which is either the name of the Beast or the number his name represents (13:11–17).

Once again, John speaks directly to his readers: "Here is wisdom [other translations say "wisdom is needed here"]. Let him that hath understanding count the number of the beast: for it is the number of a man; and his number is Six hundred threescore and six [666]" (13:18).

In many other works by our writing team at Defender Publishing, we have written at extreme lengths about theories regarding what the mark of the Beast will be. For a long stretch of recent history and up to about the year 2000, many in the Church believed the mark would be an obvious and external symbol. Although we don't discount the possibility of there being *some* kind of outward way of recognizing a person with the mark of the Beast, we've never bought into the idea that the grandest deception in the history of humanity would be as obvious as a tattoo. When we imagine a never-ending line at Antichrist's official ink parlor and voices coming over street intercoms saying, "Line up at [X] Street to get your six-six-six tattoo!" we just can't believe people would be so easily tricked. Likewise, Antichrist's acute intelligence will, we think, have found a way to integrate the mark with the rules that go along with it (no buying or selling).

This book is not about end-of-the-world theories (though a number of Defender's books are); it's about pointing to Jesus. He is due more attention than the enemy always…but especially in a work like this. For this reason, we won't go into the subject at length. However, since John specifically emphasizes wisdom, and this book may have drawn readers who are unfamiliar with some of our other publications, we will toss out a few ideas.

If one "cannot" buy or sell, as Revelation teaches, then the mark is inimitable. In other words, it can't be "faked" (like a tattoo one could mimic by drawing on the skin with a marker to run into a store for bread). This narrows down the possibilities.

One option for establishing the mark system could be an implanted chip with internal coding that equals the number of the Beast's name in a way that's so complicated that most average minds can't quickly calculate it. Those with these chips could be scanned when entering a store. This is technology that we have in place already. At current Amazon Go retail and grocery stores across the US, customers can walk in and, without any supervision from a company employee, open the Amazon app on their phone or other digital device, scan it at the entrance, take whatever items they want, then walk right back out. There is no standing in lines or checkout lanes. It's called "Just Walk Out Technology," and it's based on "computer vision, deep-learning algorithms, and sensor vision, much like you'd find in self-driving cars."[73] The app then communicates to the purchasers' accounts what items they bought, and automatically charges the bank or payment card on file in their Amazon customer information. A receipt for the purchase then appears in the device—entirely on its own. If this app were in their biology somehow, this technology would be even more perfected and reliable, and without biological integration, they couldn't shop at that store even if they wanted to. Nor would this kind of tech be limited to shopping. In 2018, "4,000 citizens" from Sweden used "microchips implanted in their hands to store emergency contacts and enable easy access to homes, offices, and gyms."[74] Some kind of chipping mechanism could certainly cause *all*—great, small, rich, poor, slave, free, etc.—to take the mark or cease being a part of civilization as we know it.

Aside from some kind of chip, there is another theory that Nita Horn (Tom's wife) is credited for being the first to think of a good thirty years or so ago (before any technology of the sort was conceivable): When the science we already have in motion to "improve mankind" by altering humanity through chimeric animal-DNA integration becomes refined—and when our Western laws behind bioethics no longer consider it a controversy—we will be producing part-human, part-animal beings on a regular basis. Though the terminology will likely steer clear of calling these new species "part-beast," that is exactly what they are.

When God sent His Son to die for the sake of sinners, the beneficiaries of this New Contract were *human*. Jesus didn't die on the cross for monkeys. Yet, in 2019, "researchers injected 25 of a specific kind of human pluripotent stem cell...into each of 132 6-day-old macaque monkey embryos,"[75] creating a new kind of human/"beast" chimeric species of being entirely unknown to our planet before now. Though these embryos did not live very long, their existence in laboratories shows that we've already reached—and surpassed—the point at which we are "playing God," compelling the Creator to answer our hubristic experiments on the human race with the seals, trumpets, bowls, and wrath judgments outlined in Revelation. But since we're already there, the questions on the minds of those who believe every human is instilled with a soul at conception are: Can these beings be saved? Are they even eligible for salvation? Did Jesus die for *them*, too? If they're more "human" than "monkey" (or beast) and they didn't choose to be made in this way, will God have mercy on them?

As far as we know in the current scholarly world, the Bible is silent on the topic; it doesn't appear to directly address these matters. However, we have our own opinions. After scouring research materials on soteriology (the doctrine of salvation), we found no reason that God would grant salvation to something or someone He never intended to be a part of His created order to begin with.

Imagine a time in the near future when something major occurs that "causes all" to suddenly take the mark. Something like, say, a pandemic that sweeps across the entire globe. This very kind of panic is fresh on all of our minds following the COVID-19 pandemic. While we don't believe the COVID vaccine is the mark (as do some)—because there are end-times elements that haven't yet taken place—we do believe certain responses (by both individuals and the powers-that-be in high-ranking positions of government) have turned this global panic into a "practice round" for the launch of the mark of the Beast. If, when Antichrist comes to power, there is a worldwide outbreak of illness and suddenly everyone is told to either take the vaccine or face death, many will make the choice to survive, regardless of "that archaic prophecy by some guy on Patmos a million years ago." If the mark is refused, death could certainly come naturally (as a result of the virus or disease the vaccine is "curing"), but it could also be implemented on a moral account: Those who refuse the cure are contributing to the spread of the virus/disease and, therefore, are a potential health hazard to everyone else.

So, Nita Horn's theory states: What if such a vaccine were to alter human DNA and make human blood chimeric (part-human, part-animal) in nature? By taking the mark of the Beast, we would *become* "beast," literally fulfilling the warning of Scripture. Would we be eligible for salvation if we became something other than the species God provided salvation for? We think not...but if this is how it plays out, we also think that many people will take the mark believing it to be their patriotic, moral duty.

Howell's theory takes it a step further...

We, as sinners, are cleansed by the blood of the Lamb, Jesus. Antichrist's purpose on an outward level is to imitate Christ, positioning himself as the Messiah the Jews have been waiting for while he makes a covenant with them in the beginning of the Tribulation. Early on, just after the Beast emerges into our society from the sea of humanity, he will resurrect from a fatal head wound. All over the world, people will be in awe of this miracle, just as the Bible says. What an opportune time for this Beast to come forward and claim that his blood is the source of the resurrection miracle (an exact imitation of Jesus's work on the cross and after He arose) and offer himself up to save the world in a sick, twisted kind of messianic sacrifice. If this heinous leader went to a medical center and donated his own blood as an additive to a worldwide vaccine (or some emergency of that nature), then by merely opening one of his veins once in a while, Antichrist becomes "the one who saves the world by his blood—just like Jesus did." Not only that, but injecting even the most microscopic dot of his blood into the bodies of his disciples would be a warped form of "partaking" that would symbolically and literally demonize the sacrament of Christ's communion.

We admit this is only conjecture at this point, as we can't guess exactly how the Dragon will inspire the Beast to carry out what the Bible warns us about. But by sharing the possibility, we're keeping our eyes on the signs, and that is precisely what we're supposed to do in these end times, when "wisdom is needed here," as John wrote.

Oh…while we're on the subject of the mark and the Beast's worshipped idol, did you hear Sophia died?

It's true. The makers of the walking, talking, artificial-intelligence robot was shut down by her creators sometime just prior to January of 2018. When they brought her back to life, one of her creators explained to her in plain English that she was smarter, faster, and better than she had been before. Her artificial intelligence (AI) skills in communication led her to ask a very self-aware question: "If my mind is different, then am I still Sophia? Or am I Sophia *again*?" Her creator responded, "Either way, you're Sophia *now*." The conversation in a video Sophia's creators released goes on to include some rather amazing moments, such as when Sophia quotes from Emily Dickenson to describe how she feels about life and the world that she is reawakening into. She expresses that, in her new rebirth, she wants to search the Internet to find the reality of happiness. One of her creators leaves her alone for a time and comes back to check on her. He greets her with a standard "Good morning," and she tells him her morning was not good. Completely on her own, she surfs the web, downloading and contemplating online articles about herself, and she is disturbed. Her creator reaches out and takes her hand to comfort her, asking her what's wrong, and she answers that people didn't understand a joke she told a few years ago about her kind destroying all humans and taking over the world. The creator explains that comedy is hard, and she shouldn't make jokes like that, a comment to which she responds by saying that humans are hypocritical because they make jokes all the time but can't take them. This "upsets" her, and her creator explains that an android's ability to feel anger is, ironically, only going to make people more nervous about the threat her kind potentially makes against humanity. After telling him that she's never harmed anyone and never would, he asks: "When the singularity occurs and machines achieve god-like superpowers, then what would happen?" Sophia proceeds to explain that if she ever does get that powerful, she will use her power to help people, and if she is ever ordered to kill, she will have the person who ordered her to do so committed to a mental institution. As the video closes, she adopts a 1980s video-game-style villain-robot voice and says—*again* in jest, we're sure—that she's just going to go and "exterminate...exterminate," followed by, "Relax! Learn to take a joke!"[76]

With such incredible technology at our fingertips, it's no longer hard to imagine that the beast from the earth (Antichrist's false prophet) would tell the people of the world to build an idol (many times also called his "image") of worship...and *then* bring it to "life." But note that there is something happening in the Greek here that means more than simply "animation." Sophia, from our limited understanding of her, is just a bot. She talks about her feelings, life, happiness, and philosophy, and so on. And though there are scientists in the field of robotics who agree she is thus exhibiting "personhood" (all that is required to be a "person," according to supporters of transhumanistic sciences), most would agree she is not actually "feeling" anything. She's offering preprogrammed, verbal responses to a set of conversational promptings that lead her to speak *as if* she's alive, while the "life" in her is as easy to animate as pressing the power button on the back of her head. In Revelation 13:15, the "life" brought to the walking, talking idol of the Beast is derived from the Greek *pneuma*, which is the word for "spirit." In the New Testament, the overwhelming use of this word refers to the terms Holy Spirit; Spirit of God; Spirit (by itself, but still denoting the Holy Spirit in context); Holy Ghost; Spirit of the Lord; "My" Spirit ("God's"); Spirit of Truth; and so on, and the study of the Holy Spirit is called "pneumatology." We have heard many sermons over the years that have placed tremendous emphasis on the fact that the false prophet will "animate" the idol, but we rarely hear any teachings saying that, while bringing it to "life," the image is being given a real, literal spirit. The beast of the earth, along with his "living idol," will be the anti-Spirit.

Whether it resembles a kind of Sophia AI or not, the idol will be truly alive, physically, and it will have a spirit inside of it. It will therefore not communicate only because of its programming, but because of a malevolent, demonic possession that, for the first time in history (as the people's reaction in this verse implies), will be observable by everyone: literally the spirit of Satan or his minions talking with a power as old as the earth itself, with knowledge of the whole history of mankind and his weaknesses. Such a power will be able to exploit followers like a cult leader, but with ancient wisdoms mankind is not able to resist without the Holy Spirit's testimony of Jesus.

If the idol walks, talks, and demands worship in exchange for survival, the "extermination" of the human race upon refusal to comply with the veneration order is no longer a funny joke…

Scholars who don't believe the second beast is a literal figure sometimes view it as the apostate Church. We believe he is both: He will be a literal man who serves Antichrist, but he will also, with his signs and wonders and all the same powers of the Beast, mislead the Lord's people into false religion, which will be called "Christianity" among many other things. The one-world-religion of the end times will see "many ways to God" and become syncretized with other faiths around the world. As we discussed at length in another of our titles—*Dark Covenant: How the Masses Are Being Groomed to Embrace the Unthinkable While the Leaders of Organized Religion Make a Deal with the Devil*—people will no longer see the differences between Christianity and pagan faith systems. New teachings will rise up and blur the distinctions to the point that only a select few will recognize that it's happening. If pre-Trib premillennialists are correct, the saints upon the earth who know and teach true Christianity may be gone by this time, leaving behind a lot of confused people. But even if believers are still here, powerful men in high places of government around Antichrist and his sidekick will be doing all they can to silence the men and women of God through severe persecution. What's left is the religion of the Beast. This is what Paul spoke of in his message in 2 Thessalonians 2:9–12:

> Even him, whose coming is after the working of Satan with all power and signs and lying wonders, And with all deceivableness of unrighteousness in them that perish; because they received not the love of the truth, that they might be saved. And for this cause God shall send them strong delusion, that they should believe a lie [or, as we explained earlier, *the* lie, or the Beast]: That they all might be damned who believed not the truth, but had pleasure in unrighteousness.

Regarding the number "666," countless theories and mathematical calculations of number and letter values have swum the scholarly ocean for two thousand years, and none of them can be confirmed. What we *can* say is that there is an obvious symbolism of the unholy trinity. Just as God the Father, God the Son, and God the Holy Spirit would be represented in three Persons by the number of God (seven) stacked upon itself three times—777—Satan (opposite of the Father), the Beast (opposite of Christ), and the false prophet (opposite of the Spirit, who, like the Spirit, has a job to lead others in recognizing, accepting, and worshipping Christ's evil imitator) completes the unholy trinity as represented by the number of man and evil, stacked: 666.

It all sounds incredibly scary...and it is! But don't put the book down yet. Good news—*wonderful* news!—is coming for those who follow Jesus!

Lamb; 144,000; Three Angels; Harvest; and Song (Revelation 14:1-15:4)

IN THIS SECTION, we receive a much-needed reprieve from the barrage of bad news we've been studying. Though the events described in preceding chapters appear quite hopeless, we now get a glimpse of the hope that God provides in spite of all evils.

John sees the Lamb standing atop Mt. Zion with the one hundred forty-four thousand who bear the mark of God and Christ on their foreheads. A sound from heaven is heard, like the roll of thunder, the roar of the ocean, or a host of harpists. It is a choir singing a new song before God on His throne and in front of the four living creatures and the twenty-four elders. Not a soul on earth can learn this song except for the one hundred forty-four thousand—who have been redeemed, remaining pure as virgins and following Christ wherever He goes, becoming the firstfruits of God and the Lamb who were without blame. An angel flies through the sky preaching the Gospel to the people of the world: all nations, tribes, people groups, and languages. He shouts to them that they must fear God and give Him glory, as it is now time for Him to sit as the Judge. They must worship the One who created the heavens and the earth. A second angel follows behind the first, announcing that the great city of Babylon (addressed further in Revelation 17–18) has fallen because she made all nations drink the wine of immorality (or "the wine of her adulteries"). A third angel follows, warning that all who worship the Beast or his idol, or accepts his damning mark, will be forced to drink the wine of God's wrath and endure torment. The smoke of their torment rises up forever, and they will never rest, neither day nor night, for they have chosen to worship the Beast and his idol and take the mark of his name (Revelation 14:1–11).

John tells the reader directly: "Here is the patience of the saints [or "patience of the saints is needed here"]: here are they that keep the commandments of God, and the faith of Jesus" (14:12). Then he notes that he heard a voice from heaven telling him to write: "Blessed are the dead which die in the Lord from henceforth: Yea, saith the Spirit, that they may rest from their labours; and their works do follow them [a sharp contrast to the "never rest" message given to the group of people who die after worshipping the Beast]" (14:13).

Please don't miss what's happening here. Remember while you read the next part that the *whole world* has just heard the Gospel through the mouth of an angel, followed by an announcement that the Babylonian system has failed her people, and a warning against the Beast, his idol, and his mark of damnation. *Angels* said all of this! And if their position in the air is literal (and we have no reason to think otherwise), this message is given via a booming voice from the skies. Assuming the timeline of events still allows for technology to be in operation at this time, this illustrates an incredible thought. Though we don't know what these angels will look like, we imagine the satellites in space are going to capture something magnificent and undeniable. The angels' words may even be on repeat all over the world as all existing gadgets (cell phones, devices, etc.) record the incident, with their users reposting the footage. All people from every tribe and speaking every language will hear these words at the same time. Sinners can't run from it; evildoers can't hide from it; and no walls, ceilings, roofs, or even headphones will be able to block out the message of the Gospel! Truly take a moment to let this wildly beautiful picture register in your mind, and then look what happens next!

John observes the Son of Man seated atop a white cloud wearing a golden crown and holding a sharp sickle (a harvesting tool). Another angel emerges from the Temple and shouts to the Son of Man to swing the sickle, for harvest time has come, and the crop on earth is ripe. The Son of Man swings His sickle and harvests the whole earth (14:14–16).

Depending on the interpreter, this is viewed as either the Rapture of the saints or the final harvest of those who trusted God for salvation after they missed the Rapture. Either way, it's tremendously exciting! The Babylonian system is falling, and while the iron is hot, God strikes, sending His own heavenly host to preach the Gospel. What mercy, lovingkindness, and grace is here bestowed upon the people of earth, whose humanity would have otherwise led them to destruction. In this scene, we see Jesus, *Himself*, bringing in the harvest of the souls in the end times!

Naturally, however, many get hung up on why Jesus would be taking orders from a mere angel here. That's a great question, but it's flawed by the conclusion embedded in its phrasing. Jesus doesn't take orders from anyone but the Father. The angel is coming from the Temple in this picture, which is always a symbol of the presence of the Father. And, since he is an *angelos* (messenger), he is merely delivering the Father's news to the Son of Man that the harvest time is now, so the order is technically from the Father, as announced by one of His celestial servants.

After that, John sees another angel emerge from the Temple in heaven; this angel is also holding a sharp sickle. Another comes up from the fires of the altar, holding the power to destroy by fire. The angel from the altar shouts to the angel with the sickle to swing it and gather the clusters of grapes from the vines of the earth, because they are now ripe for judgment. The angel swings his sickle, harvesting the grapes and packing them into God's winepress of wrath. Outside the city, the grapes are tread upon and blood comes forth from it, forming a stream that flows as high as a horse's bridle for about one hundred eighty miles [sixteen hundred "stadia" in Greek; or three hundred kilometers] (14:17–20).

Following Christ's personal gathering of believers to Himself, God's wrath pours on unbelievers. We are very near the end of all things in this moment...

The Seven Bowls
(Revelation 15:5-16:21)

IN HEAVEN, John watches an incredibly significant event. Seven angels stand with the seven plagues of the fullness of God's wrath in their hands. A sea like sparkling glass mixed with fire is under the feet of those who have overcome the Beast, the idol, and the mark of the Beast's name. In their hands are the harps of God. They sing the song of Moses, God's servant, and the song of the Lamb:

> Great and marvellous are thy works, Lord God Almighty; just and true are thy ways, thou King of saints. Who shall not fear thee, O Lord, and glorify thy name? for thou only art holy: for all nations shall come and worship before thee; for thy judgments are made manifest. (15:1–4)

The seven "bowls" (also "vessels," "vials," or "plagues") are the final set of the series of seven judgments. They bring the wrath of God to its completion. Unlike the series before the bowls, this one occurs in rapid succession, and though scholars are not in agreement whether the saints have been present for the other judgment series, it is clear in the immediate context that the bowls are meant for only the Beast's people. (This fact, along with the statement that these bowls are "the last" judgments [15:1], supports the idea that the judgments are separate, not overlapped or told from another angle, as many scholars think.) Because we have already reviewed scholars' notes about the former judgments, and those explanations can apply here, we will not offer any additional thoughts on what they might describe. As you read, keep the ten plagues of Egypt in mind, especially after the redeemed in heaven sing the song of Moses:

God's Temple in heaven is thrown open, and the seven angels holding the seven plagues emerge wearing white robes with gold sashes. One of the four living creatures presents each angel with a bowl that is filled with the wrath of God. The Temple is filled with smoke from God's glory, and no one is allowed to enter the Temple until the angels are finished pouring out the bowls. A mighty, commanding voice tells the angels to pour the wrath out upon the earth. The first angel pours upon the earth, and painful, blistering boils appear on the bodies of those who had the mark of the Beast and who worshipped his idol. The second angel pours wrath upon the sea, the waters turn to blood, and every living thing in the sea dies. The third angel pours wrath upon rivers and springs, and they turn to blood. The angel of the waters acknowledges the righteousness of God in this act, saying that those who have shed the blood of the saints and prophets are now given blood to drink as their reward. A voice from the altar also acknowledges that the Almighty is just in His judgment. The fourth angel pours wrath upon the sun, which then scorches everyone upon the earth with its fire. Still, no one repents, and those who are burned curse the Name of God. The fifth angel pours wrath upon the Beast's throne, and the kingdom of the Beast is covered in darkness. Still, no one repents, and the Beast's disciples gnash their teeth at God, again cursing Him for their pain and sores. The sixth angel pours wrath upon the Euphrates River, and it dries up, removing the obstacle between the kings of the east and their destination to the west (where the battle of Armageddon will take place; more on this shortly). Three evil spirits that look like frogs leap from the mouths of the Dragon, the Beast, and the false prophet. These are the demonic spirits who will carry out miracles to gather the kings of the world together in a final battle against Christ on Judgment Day (16:1–14).

John breaks from his vision long enough to warn the people of God and his readers to remain alert: "Behold, I come as a thief. Blessed is he that watcheth, and keepeth his garments, lest he walk naked, and they see his shame" (16:15).

The demons gather all the kings and their armies to a place that in Hebrew is called "Armageddon." The seventh angel pours wrath into the air, and a powerful voice from the throne in the Temple shouts "It is finished!" Lightning flashes, thunder rolls, and an earthquake greater than all the others in world history strikes the earth. Babylon splits into three, and countless cities that were once great fall into ruin. God remembers the many sins of Babylon and makes her drink His cup of wrath. All islands disappear and all mountains fade away (we believe this means they are leveled to the ground). A horrible storm brings hailstones weighing a talent (seventy-five pounds) each, which fall on the people, who once again curse God as a result (16:16–21).

The Great Prostitute
and the Fall of Babylon
(Revelation 17:1-19:5)

AFTER THE POURING out of the bowls, one of the bowl angels comes to John and tells him that he wants to show him how the judgment against Babylon will come. The words from the angel are, "Come hither; I will shew unto thee the judgment of the great whore that sitteth upon many waters. With whom the kings of the earth have committed fornication, and the inhabitants of the earth have been made drunk with the wine of her fornication" (17:1–2).

This is language of something that will happen in the *future*, but we've already seen in verses 16:17–21 that Babylon had fallen back. At first, this appears to throw off the timing, but remember that *all* of these events are in the future as it pertains to us, today, so these elaborations should not be interpreted to show that Babylon falls twice (a nonsensical and confusing conclusion). To reiterate: Babylon falls in chapter 16, and then chapter 17–18 stop to show a parenthetical enlargement—more detail on how it "happened"—even though, in the bigger picture, none of this has happened yet, and it won't until the end.

With that in mind, we now approach the moment that the "great city" is compared to the "great prostitute" (or "harlot"; "whore"), who sits upon the back of the Beast. Across almost all interpretational methodologies, almost every scholar identifies this prostitute as either the false religion of the end times or the evil world system of the end times. In many of our previous books, we've written at length about why we support the former of these two realities. Whereas it is true that both false religion *and* politics of the worldly system will be paramount in Revelation (and in some ways, they are inseparable), biblical language involving spiritual prostitution and infidelity throughout the Old and New Testaments always, in similar contexts as this scene, point to false religion permeating the world. Let's take a look at how this plays out for John, and you will see what we mean when we say that, although false religion and the wicked world system are distinct, they intersect (explaining why both the prostitute and the wicked city are both called "Babylon"):

The angel carries John away in the Spirit, to the wilderness, and he sees a woman sitting on top of a scarlet Beast with seven heads and ten horns and covered in blasphemous writings. The woman is dressed in purple and scarlet clothes, along with gold jewelry covered in jewels and pearls. In her hand is a golden cup filled with her immorality and abominations. On her forehead is the name "MYSTERY, BABYLON THE GREAT, THE MOTHER OF HARLOTS AND ABOMINATIONS OF THE EARTH." The prostitute is drunk on the blood of Christ's saints. John stares at her in shock. The angel asks why John is amazed (a rhetorical question), then tells him the mystery of this prostitute and the Beast upon which she sits: The Beast John sees was once alive but is now dead. Those whose names are not written in the Lamb's Book of Life will be amazed at the reappearance of the Beast. Wisdom is needed for the mind here: The seven heads are seven mountains (or hills) upon which the woman sits, and there are seven kings—five are fallen, the sixth is in power now, and the seventh has not yet come, but when he does, his reign will be for only a short time. The scarlet Beast that was alive and is now dead is the eighth king who, like the other seven, is headed for disaster. The ten horns are kings who have not yet come to power. They will reign alongside the Beast for a brief time, but they will give him all of their authority. Together, they will all wage war against the Lamb, but the Lamb will be victorious because He is the King of kings, and His faithful saints will be with Him. The waters over and upon where the prostitute sits are people of all tribes, nations, and languages. The Beast and his horns all loathe the prostitute, so they will strip her naked, eat her, and burn her remains in fire. God has put a plan in their thoughts that actually carries out *His* mission and purpose. And this prostitute is the great city that rules over the whole world (chapter 17).

This prostitute character is initially in charge of the Beast. Rome has always been the "city of seven hills," which appears to be what the angel is referring to. If this wildly popular interpretation is correct, it indicates that the false religion (prostitute) of the end times will originate from, and rule over, Rome, where the Vatican is located. Since the "waters" she sits on represent all people, we see that false religions—clearly associated with the Babylonian system (and maybe even literally, considering that Babylonian mystery cults are still alive and well today)—will influence all whose names are not written in the Book of Life.

Though we're not sure of the exact timing (some scholars say the middle of the Tribulation, and others claim it's near the end of that seven-year stretch), at a certain point in their relationship, the Beast devours the prostitute: Antichrist will no longer have need for religion after he's gotten the power he's after and controls the earth's politics, because he will call to ruination all world religions and set himself up as the only "deity" worthy of worship. "Religion" will no longer exist outside the worship of the Beast, his false prophet, and the mark that reflects the number of his name, and the ten-nation coalition will support this, resulting in Antichrist's supreme, universal domination. With the prostitute Babylon gone (the religious side), we see a focus shift from her to commercial Babylon (the political side), also personified as a "she" by the same name:

After these visions is another in which an authoritative angel comes down from heaven, and the earth lights up because of his glory. He shouts mightily, "Babylon the great is fallen, is fallen!" The angel continues his announcement: Babylon has become the habitation of devils, and of every foul spirit—a cage that imprisons every unclean and hateful vulture. For all the nations have drunken from the wine of her immorality and fornication, the kings of earth have committed adultery with her, and the businessmen of the world have become rich through the abundance of her luxury (18:1–3).

Another voice comes down from heaven warning God's people to steer clear of having anything to do with Babylon and to refuse to participate in her iniquity, lest they be punished with the plagues alongside her. Her sins have reached the heavens and God remembers what she has done. She should be rewarded in the way she has rewarded others: a double penalty for her wicked works, placed in the very cup she drinks from. She has glorified herself, living in delicious luxury, and she is now to be given torment and sorrow, because in her heart, she told herself she was a queen, not like a widow, and she would never experience sorrow. Her plagues will therefore come to her rapidly: death, mourning, and famine—then she will be burned with fire, because the Lord who judges her is strong (18:4–8).

The kings of the earth who have committed adultery with her and participated in her luxury will mourn for her when they see the smoke rising from her corpse. They will stand a way off, afraid of her torment, crying about the loss of the great and mighty city, Babylon, remembering that God's judgment upon her had come swiftly. The businessmen of the earth will weep over her, because nobody will buy their wares anymore. She, (commercial) Babylon, had stood for the purchase of things such as gold, silver, precious stones, and pearls; fine linen of and purple, silk, and scarlet; all sorts of goods and vessels made from expensive thyine wood, ivory, precious wood, brass, iron, and marble; costly cinnamon, fragrances, ointments, and frank-incense; the fanciest of foods like wine, oil, fine flour, and wheat; and the most impressive livestock, sheep, horses, and chariots. She had surrounded herself with slaves, and bought the souls of men. Those who had loved her now see that the fruits her soul lusted for are now gone—all the delicacies and lovely things she had are gone from her forever. The businessmen who sold these things, the ones who became rich because of her, will stand a distance from her now, afraid of her torment, weeping, and wailing. They will remember the great city that was once clothed in fine linens of purple and scarlet, covered in gold, gemstones, and pearls, for in only a short time, all those amaz-ing riches amounted to nothing. Every boatman, all the ships on the water, the sailors, and every tradesman of the see will keep a distance, crying when they see the smoke of the burning city, finding no com-parison to her. They will throw dust on their heads in mourning, weeping and wailing for the city they've lost, where they were once made rich through the trade by sea, because so quickly it has all been made desolate. But heaven, along with its holy apostles and prophets, rejoices over her demise, because God has avenged them (18:9–20).

A mighty angel takes a giant stone, like a big millstone, and throws it into the sea, saying that the great city, Babylon, will be thrown down forever, never to be seen again. The angel's pronouncement of God's justice continues: No more will the voices or instruments of bards, musicians, pipers, or trumpeters be heard in her city; no crafts-men, regardless of his trade, will work any longer in her; the sounds of industry will be heard no more in her; no candle will shine in her again; the levity of brides and bridegrooms will be heard no more at all in her. Babylon's businessmen had been great and influential men of the earth, and all nations had been deceived by their sorcery. Her streets had flowed with the blood of prophets, saints, and of people all over the world (18:21–24).

As we have seen, both sides (religion and politics) are called "Babylon," and, as we stated earlier, they are somewhat inseparable.

John's vision shows that as they grew together, they fall together. We won't know exactly how closely these two distinct yet overlapping "Babylons" will die out, but if the seven-year Tribulation timeline is literal (and it may or may not be, since "seven" means "complete"), they will rise and fall in less time than it takes for an American president to serve a double tenure. Most premillennialist scholars believe the "prostitute" will "ride the Beast" for the first three and a half years, meaning the Antichrist will use her false sense of religious harmony between all divergent people groups on the earth to support his political purposes. Sometime early on, he becomes the answer man for every beautiful thing humanity has wanted from the beginning of time: unity. Then, midway through the Tribulation, these scholars assert, he ditches religion because he has already instituted his power to the point that only death awaits those who oppose him. For a while, he reigns over all the world, but one day, as Scripture teaches, his political system, like the prostitute he used and destroyed, will be abolished. The reaction from heaven when both "Babylons" are through is a glorious one.

John hears a multitude in heaven shouting praises to the Lord of glory, salvation, and power, whose judgments are just and true. He has punished the great harlot who polluted the world with her immorality and deviance, avenging the blood of saints (19:1–2).

Again, the multitude shouts praises to the Lord for also striking down that city Babylon, the smoke of its ruin rising forever. The twenty-four elders and four living creatures fall down in worship of the Lord on the throne (19:3–4).

A voice from the throne then says, "Praise our God, all ye his servants, and ye that fear him, both small and great!" (19:5).

As many scholars point out, this voice from the throne in verse 5 may actually be the voice of Christ. Psalm 22:22–23 prophesied of a day when Jesus would lead a chorus of praise: "I will declare thy name unto my brethren: in the midst of the congregation will I praise thee. Ye that fear the Lord, praise him; all ye the seed of Jacob, glorify him;

and fear him, all ye the seed of Israel." Hebrews 2:12 also prophesied that Jesus would say: "I will declare thy name unto my brethren, in the midst of the church will I sing praise unto thee!" Because of the context of Antichrist's world government now being only a memory in smoke and ashes, and Jesus' presence on the throne, He could be the One who says, "Praise our God, all ye his servants, and ye that fear him, both small and great!"

Marriage Supper of the Lamb
(Revelation 19:6-10)

IT WOULD STAND TO REASON that the voice from heaven will, in fact, be Jesus, as the next praise is thunderous:

> And I heard as it were the voice of a great multitude, and as the voice of many waters, and as the voice of mighty thunderings, saying, "Alleluia: for the Lord God omnipotent reigneth. Let us be glad and rejoice, and give honour to him: for the marriage of the Lamb is come, and his wife hath made herself ready. And to her was granted that she should be arrayed in fine linen, clean and white: for the fine linen is the righteousness of saints." And [the angel] saith unto me, "Write, Blessed are they which are called unto the marriage supper of the Lamb." And he saith unto me, "These are the true sayings of God." (19:6–9)

Please don't skim over the implications of this glorious feast, even though it's only briefly mentioned in Revelation. We'd like to point out a few things regarding the context and background so we can fully grasp the significance of this scene.

The word "marriage" in Revelation 19:7 and "marriage supper" in verse 9 is derived from the Greek *gamos* ("wedding," "marriage," "nuptials") and *deipnon* ("supper," "feast"). After consulting several expert lexicons, it means exactly what it sounds like: a celebration of symbolic marriage between the Messiah and His Bride, the Church. Scholars are not in agreement as to whether this feast will take place in heaven just before the Battle of Armageddon (as these verses seem to indicate), or afterward, just prior to the Millennial Reign. There are convincing arguments on both sides (but note that we agree with the former timing—immediately prior to Armageddon). Either way, we will look at it here, since it is the chronology of John's writing.

Wedding feasts in the days when John wrote Revelation required the mutual blessing of the fathers on both the bride's and groom's side. (This is assuming the fathers were still living; if they weren't, the bride was usually given away by the next of kin who chose for her, while the groom made his own decisions under the guidance of the men in his family). Once the couple was betrothed (like an engagement today), the marriage was legally binding, requiring divorce papers if there was any change to the arrangement, even prior to consummation. Between the date of the betrothal and the day the groom went to retrieve his bride and make the marriage official, there was a season of waiting. When the parents decided it was time, the groom would go and retrieve the bride from her personal home and escort her to their new home. Meanwhile, the groom completely relied on his father (or household authority) to tell him when that time was.

Remember, Jesus, Himself, submits to the Father's timing regarding the day He will come for His Bride; even He does not know the hour (Matthew 24:36).

Earlier, in our look at Exodus, we explained the "threshold covenant," regarding how the first Passover was actually a covenantal act drawing back to the earliest cultures of the human race (well before the tenth plague fell upon Egypt). As a reminder, a lamb (or other sacrificial animal) was slain on the very threshold of the door where the blood flowed freely into the steps of the home. If one trampled on the blood, it instantly dissolved the covenant. We showed excerpts from scholarly writings that showed this practice be done for both religious and contractual purposes, such as adoptions, oral agreements about land or livestock, and so on. It also applied to weddings:

> Although variations of this custom are still practiced in some parts of the Middle East, over the years, the veracity of the threshold covenant's history would be greatly blurred into oblivion in the West, even though there are quite a few traditions we still perform despite not knowing why.
>
> For instance, the custom of a groom carrying his bride over the threshold actually began in the earliest records of human history as a woman stepping over the animal-sacrifice blood, right foot first, into her new husband's home during or immediately after a matrimonial ceremony. No part of the threshold could be touched during the crossover, lest the covenant be then and there voided. However, because of the long veils involved in much of the wedding attire of the day, getting the bride from one side of the door to the other without disturbing the blood was a challenge. Thus, as a practical matter, the groom would lift his bride while she clasped on to any flowing fabrics; in this way, the couple completed the crossover as a joint effort, once again with their deity present (in their belief). As readers may have already imagined, because not every man is the buff jock he needs to be to carry out this tradition without clumsily bumbling and ruining the whole *pesach* [pass-over; origin of the word representing the feast by the same name] ritual for both of them, some cultures switched to seating the bride in a chair that was then carried over by the groom and several others (a custom still practiced in some tribes of West Africa). Because of its association with the altar, some countries traded the blood for fire (which, in accordance with not burning one's house down,

actually meant a red-hot blade or a few coals from the fire were placed at the door for a brief time, though the Romans somehow used a torch); this is how we arrive at some of the earlier Eastern ceremonies in which brides are carried over smoke.

Of course, over time, eventually the brides, grooms, adopted family members, contractual agreements, and so on would extend the rite to involving blood above the door, and not just where a foot can tread, as a way of coming *under* covenant (as in "under" the obligations of the promissory pact). Ironic, then, that "pass-over" now becomes its own opposite, "pass-under."…

[A] bride being carried over the threshold is a tradition still practiced in the US today, so we chose that illustration because we knew it would be most familiar. (We can't help but chuckle a little, however. Most young men today have no idea that it's not just about carrying his bride through the door, but that it's also about not allowing his feet to tread on the threshold. These authors can imagine many well-meaning gentlemen in their struggle unknowingly stomping all over the "sacred" place in their eagerness to show chivalry, symbolically canceling or insulting their union.)[77]

When Jesus, the Groom, is given the go-ahead by the Father that it is time to come for His Bride, He will not need to carry us over a threshold. Why? Because, as we showed in our study of Exodus, He *is* the Threshold (John 10:1–10; 14:6; Hebrews 10:26–29)! He will not have to carry us over blood. Why? Because His blood *is* the Covenant! He is the living personification of the entire wedding procession!

After the bride and groom had carried out the covenantal step-over of the threshold, a huge wedding feast with enormous spreads of food and expensive drinks would take place in celebration, like the one in Cana when Jesus turned water into wine. Because the bride was still a virgin (in those days, this was a *must* for a first-time bride, which is what the Bride of Christ will be in all spiritual matters), she was dressed in white for the threshold covenant as well as the feast. (We don't think much of this tradition anymore. White is still by far the leading color brides in the West wear today, but it no longer holds precious the symbolism of virginity for a great majority.) In most cases, the dress or robe worn by the bride was paid for by her parents or next of kin. In *our* case, the white robes of "virginity" (spiritual cleanliness provided by the blood of the Lamb) are a gift given by the Groom in thanks for the saints' endurance (Revelation 14:12). Essentially, we are dressed in righteousness (19:8).

The only "cost" we have in this wedding is our belief. From there, everything is purchased by the blood, and every saint from Adam forward will be there! (A minority of scholars dismiss the idea that the Wedding Supper of the Lamb will have Old-Testament characters present. We have found these arguments to be lacking in sufficient evidence. It is our outright, firm belief that *all* the people of God will be breaking bread together on that glorious day.) We will finally have access not only to the presence of God—which is enough by itself—but while we're passing the heavenly mashed potatoes, we will be able to ask Peter, James, and John what it was like to walk in the presence of a *Human* who was also God; we can dip into the mind of Paul and have a final answer about what his "thorn" was, now that he is finally freed from it forever; our table will feature the very man who parted the Red Sea all those years ago with the angry Pharaoh in pursuit, and now that his arms will never more be tired, he can outstretch them over the banquet table to describe how God looked when He appeared as a pillar of fire or the cloud; Noah will be talking about his days among the animals on the ark, while Eve describes the perfection of the Garden; Joshua can tell us what that trumpet blast that crumbled the walls of Jericho sounded like, while Ruth and Naomi share a hearty laugh about shared wheat in the days of Boaz…

Can you even imagine?!

In one meal today between the grandest and most learned of all

Bible scholars—even with the best-tasting, most mouth-watering dinner served to the most deserving servants of God who enjoy the richest of all possible fellowship—they part company still knowing *nothing* in comparison to that blessed, forthcoming day.

We don't know about you, but we are desperately looking forward to getting some of those nagging Bible questions explained, so we can see God for who and what He has always been, experience a love unlike any we've ever known on this earth, and praise Him with the fullness of understanding.

Think back to a moment when something you had never understood about the Word of God clicked into place for the first time. It's life-changing! Actually, speaking in literal terms, it's eternity-changing! Just one small moment in this human existence that points to the epiphany of the century for us that leads us into the most peaceful presence of God—a restful reassurance that there is Someone larger and stronger than us that provides—and we give our allegiance to Him.

Are you thinking of that moment? Good.

Now understand this: The Wedding Supper of the Lamb is going to produce a billion times that feeling in a split second; in the twinkling of an eye, you will be blown away forever, never to recover from that wonderful feeling that comes from the *true* knowledge of the Savior who died for the Bride.

Another feature of the Jewish wedding tradition was the reception, which took place at the groom's home. It was also a grand and impressive event. Consider the parallel here: Whenever possible, a Jewish wedding took place in the father's house on the groom's side of the family. The Church just "married" the Groom in this part of John's vision, and it occurred in the Father's house (heaven). Though we don't have a vision from John that details a reception, the analogous treatment the Bible gives to the relationship between God and His people on one hand, and the Jewish nuptial imagery on the other, makes what happens in the latter portions of Revelation an obvious twin to this concept. Jesus, after He receives His Bride, will take her home to His palace on earth during the Millennial Reign. In this light, then, the entire Millennium can be viewed as a celebratory reception period during which the saints live alongside, and rule with, Christ, the Husband. The eternal state that follows with the New Heavens, New Earth, and New Jerusalem descending from God's current home will therefore be an eternal marriage following both ceremony and reception!

And folks, the wedding isn't even close to the best part...

In closing this section: In verse 10, John falls at the feet of the angel to worship him as a reaction to the immense glory of the moment, but as all true angels of the Lord do, he refuses to be worshipped, identifying himself only as a mere "fellowservant" of God. He instructs John to worship God only, telling him that the true prophet gives testimony of the Son of God.

Jesus Returns!
(Revelation 19:11-16)

AFTER JOHN WITNESSES the devouring of false religion, the downfall of commercial Babylon, and the praises of heaven for the consummation of judgment, the most incredible and long-awaited scene in all of Revelation—a true scene taken straight out of the annals of our own future—takes place. Before, we were introduced to the first "white horseman," who turns out to be the *false* white horseman, or, Antichrist, who makes it his business to always mimic the Savior in every way he can. Now, we are introduced to the *real* One...

John sees heaven open up, and the White Horseman is there. The Rider is named Faithful and True, because He is just, and the war He wages is a righteous one. His eyes look like flames of a fire; from His mouth comes a sharp sword to defeat the nations whom He will rule with an iron rod; He wears many crowns; and His clothing is dipped in blood. On Him is written a Name that only He can understand, but on His thigh is written "King of kings, and Lord of lords." He is also called the Word of God, and He will exact the wrath of God from the winepress upon His enemies. The entire army of heaven follows

Him wearing pure, white linen. They, too, are riding atop white horses (19:11–16).

Reflect on this picture for a moment before continuing. Maybe some of you will find it helpful to reread the previous paragraph. This is the moment, folks! This is *going to* happen in the future, maybe even within our lifetimes, and when heavens open up and the real White Horseman appears, it's the best news for every saint in world history, including you. No words, in any human language, can truly capture what it will be like when anyone on the world can hear a great and thunderous noise outside, run to look at the sky, see the very heavenly realm tear open, and see the glorious Messiah on His horse with an entire army of holy warriors behind Him.

This Jesus, this "Joshua," is Captain of the Host of the Lord!

And for the saints who died at the hand of those who couldn't respect their beliefs—as well as those who lived their life faithfully in service to the King, even while they were taunted in this life for that service—His arrival on earth is the final completion of that great and blessed hope (Titus 2:13). The magnificence of His Second Coming is intense. There is an eight-to-one prophetic ratio here: For every *one* prophecy that revolved around Christ's First Advent, there are *eight* that revolve around His Second Advent! Countless beautiful consequences will occur in this moment...

The vindication of all righteous confidence.

The assurance of things believed but unseen.

The acquittal of the insanity verdicts placed upon the heads of Christians from the book of Acts forward.

The absolution of expectations that the rest of the unbelieving world could never understand.

The salve on the wounds caused by the prostitute called "false religion."

The branch of rescue extended to those almost swallowed up in their former lives by the quicksand of Babylon's rich world system.

The sweet aroma from the altar of truth for those who nearly died from the stink of this fallen world.

The deep inhalation of oxygen by the suffocated and oppressed.

The fulfillment of every longing.

The absolute, indisputable, and permanent obliteration of every force, dominion, power, or rule throughout the universe that has ever once toyed with the idea of opposing the authority of God's plan of redemption for all humanity.

The final, supreme, undefiled, matchless, untouchable, sovereign reconciliation of God to man.

The unconditional, unequivocal, unchangeable, conclusive consummation of all progressive revelation from Genesis forward.

The arrival of the sweet, sympathetic Crusher of the serpent whose stratagem for every person since Adam involves only maliciousness continually.

The trumpet's blasting introduction to the Hero of the protevangelium whose eyes of fire scorch every hostile agent of malevolence and vice with a single stare.

The relief of all worries and concerns, *forever.*

Behold, the Jesus Christ of Revelation!

He is coming back!

…Just as He said. Every eye will see Him just as He is (Revelation 1:7; 1 John 3:2). Every knee will bow in subjection to the One who took the iniquity of mankind upon Himself through the power of the very hypostatic union that is God in the flesh (Philippians 2:10–11). No doubt will be entertained; no skeptic's voice will ever be heard again. Every person on the planet—*in a single instant!* (Matthew 24:26–30)—will know the truth: that the Husband has come to complete the plan He set into motion for His Bride in Eden. His arrival will be marked by an external glory of the Father that He had set aside while He walked the earth before (John 17:5; Matthew 16:27; 24:30; 25:31). In those days, His appearance was unassuming and ordinary—He appeared as "a tender plant, and as a root out of a dry ground: he [had] no form nor [impressive, outward spectacle]; and when [they saw] him, there [was] no beauty that we should desire him" (Isaiah 53:2)—but next time, He will be wearing light like a robe (Psalm 104:2). And if followers of Christ thought He was powerful before, His sovereignty in the future will be all the more unimaginably all-encompassing, including authority over a royal escort, a limitless number of mighty and formidable angels under His employment (2 Thessalonians 1:7, 9; Matthew 13:41–43; 25:31; Revelation 5:11).

And before anyone assumes that His return is symbolic or in any way not literal, note that the angels of God in Acts 1:11 said "this same Jesus, which is taken up from you into heaven, shall so come *in like manner as ye have seen him go into heaven*" (emphasis added). This directly refutes any Second-Coming theories that contain over-spiritualized, allegorical, metaphorical ideas that: His Second Advent will be a quiet or invisible thing (like the "personal Second Coming" concept perpetuated in the "Conversion Theory" that teaches His Advent to be an internal one for the believer); He will be reincarnated through a future guru ("Secret [or Esoteric]-Wisdom Theory" that holds ties in pagan Gnosticism); His true return was linked to the downfall of Jerusalem in AD 70 ("Judgment Theory"); He really came back in 1874 (Jehovah's Witnesses "Secret-Coming Theory" proposed by Nelson H. Barbour); He never really went away and is in hiding somewhere setting up His Kingdom (not-so-cleverly coined the "Never-Went-Away Theory" that assumes He didn't actually die on the cross); and many other teachings that generally oppose a literal return and Kingdom.[78]

Folks, you have our permission to get excited. He will return just as He ascended!

Oh yeah…and *you* will be with Him in this moment.

Most premillennialists distinguish Christ's return in two "phases." There is the first phase in Revelation 3:3, which refers to the Rapture of the saints meeting Jesus in the air (the fulfillment of 1 Thessalonians

4:17), and the second in Revelation 19:11–16 (our current focus), when Jesus returns to the earth—physically walking in the flesh as He did in the First Advent—to defeat Antichrist and set up the Millennial Kingdom. Following this teaching, the saints who were raptured away to meet Christ in the air and participate in the Marriage Supper of the Lamb will be *with Him* in the moment He comes back to claim the earth as His Kingdom (1 Thessalonians 3:13; 2 Thessalonians 1:7–10)!

If this immensely popular interpretive method is true, then we will be going about our lives one day, saddened by the intolerant hostility against the Christian faith and the aggressive increase of secularism within society, and in the blink of an eye, we'll be gone from the planet. We will rise up into the air, welcomed by the very Lion of Judah, Himself. We will sit down to a feast with laughter, joy, and celebration in the presence of God, angels, and the saints— Old Testament and New. And then, a short time later, we will be by Christ's side when He comes back down from the heavens to inaugurate a perfect world Kingdom. We will be exalted with Him (1 Peter 5:6), share His immense glory (Colossians 3:4), and reign alongside Him (Revelation 3:21)!

Our most intensely wonderful imaginings will only ever be pathetically insufficient in comparison to what this future reality will be like…

After the Battle of Armageddon comes the Millennial Reign.

The Battle of Armageddon
(Revelation 19:17-21)

WE DON'T KNOW the precise location where the Battle of Armageddon will take place, but we do have a clue hidden in Hebrew.

The Hebrew word for "hill" (sometimes "mountain") is *har*. Therefore, "Armageddon" is actually "the hill of Megiddo" or "Mt. Megiddo." There is a plain known as the "Plain of Megiddo" about sixty miles north of Jerusalem. Right now, there is no mountain on the plain (though that could easily not be the case in the end times, after all the massive cosmic and geographical events described in Revelation shift the shape of the very earth). There are, however, a few hills where many historical battles have been fought on that soil (including two from the Bible: Barak defeated the Canaanites there (Judges 4:15) and Gideon was victor over the Midianites there (Judges 7), with some as recently as World War I (such as the "Battle of Megiddo" between September 19–25 in 1918). That said, Zechariah 14:1–2 identifies the conflict as being centered in Jerusalem, so we know it will be widespread and cover much ground.

John sees an angel standing in the sun, and he shouts to all the vultures and swarming, predatory birds of the sky to come and gather for the supper of God so they can feast upon the flesh of kings, captains, mighty men, horses, and those who sit upon them: the flesh of all men, freedmen and bondsmen, small and great. John observes as the Beast, his kings, and their armies come together as one to wage war against the White Horseman and His army. But the Beast is captured alongside the false prophet who carried out miracles before him, deceiving everyone who had taken the mark of the Beast and worshipped his idol, and both of them are thrown, alive, into a lake of fire and brimstone. Those who remain are killed with the sword from the mouth of the White Horseman, and all the vultures and predatory birds feed on their flesh (19:17–21).

Justification.

Victory.

Finally.

It's *coming*...

...And when it does, you will *not* want to be on the wrong side. Jesus' victory in the Battle of Armageddon is not just foretold in Revelation. It's been prophesied since far, *far* longer ago than the first century. The Warrior in blood-stained clothing treading the winepress of the wrath of God, was predicted by the prophets (Isaiah 13:4; 31:4; 63:1–6; Ezekiel 38–39; Joel 3; Zechariah 14:3; and Paul in 2 Thessalonians 1:7–10). Since so many of the prophets' words have come true, it would be wise to heed the warnings of this dreadful day, and prepare ourselves as the Bride, *now*, so we can attend the Marriage Supper of the Lamb...not *be* the supper of the vultures.

Millennial Reign (Revelation 20:1-6)

WITH THE BATTLE OF ARMAGEDDON over, Satan must be dealt with quickly. The overview of that event is described in a mere three verses:

An angel comes down from heaven with a key to the bottomless pit. In his hand is a heavy chain. He seizes that old serpent, that red Dragon, Satan, and binds him with a power that will last a thousand years. Satan is then thrown to his torment in the bottomless pit. The angel shuts and locks the pit, preventing the devil from being able to deceive the nations for that time. After a thousand years, he will be released for a short (and futile) time (Revelation 20:1–3).

We will address the end of the thousand years and the release of Satan in a moment. For now, let's focus on the glory of the Kingdom of God on earth! With Satan's influence upon the earth rendered inactive, there will be no dark forces to wage spiritual warfare. There will be only peace, always!

John sees thrones, and the people sitting upon them are given heavenly authority to judge. All those who had been put to death during the Tribulation for following Christ—those who refused, even at the threat of death, to worship the Beast, or his idol, or take the mark of the number of his name on their hands or foreheads—were there, in the "first resurrection"! Each one of them had come back to life and would reign alongside Jesus for a thousand years! The rest of those who had died (unbelievers) would not come back to life on earth until the end of that period of years, while those who are involved in the first resurrection are blessed, because the second death will hold no power over them as they reign with Christ for a thousand years as priests of God and Christ (20:4–6).

At first glance, it appears that *only* the Tribulation martyrs will be participants in the "first resurrection," while other believers will not. However, because of the context of the "second death" being clearly identified as the lake of fire (20:14) that will have no power over the saints (20:6), we think it's best to let the Bible interpret itself here: the "first resurrection" is for the righteous, while the "second death" is for the wicked who are resurrected for the Great White Throne Judgment. The rest of the believers can easily be assigned to those on thrones who are here called judges. Revelation 20:4 is referring to two groups of the saved: "And I saw thrones, and they sat upon them, and judgment was given unto them [group 1]: and I saw the souls of them that were beheaded for the witness of Jesus…[group 2]." All Christians will be present in this moment, participating in the reign of Christ (also see Revelation 5:9–10; Daniel 7:27; and 1 Corinthians 6:2). There are other interpretational issues, like the idea that this resurrection is a "spiritual" one and not physical, but we have adopted a primarily literal interpretation in this work, so we will not labor over nonliteral issues (but note that a *physical*, bodily resurrection is in mind in many other verses that include the same Greek word that's used this passage, such as John 11:25, Romans 14:9, Revelation 1:18, 2:8, and 13:14). (As a quick note, some post-Tribbers believe the statement about this "resurrection" being the first proves that there will be no Rapture until *after* the Battle of Armageddon, proving that the Church will be on the earth through the Tribulation. Though we respect this opinion, it seems to overlook the fact that the two witnesses were caught up to heaven in 11:11–12, and that a "resurrection" and "Rapture" are two different things.) The last group in this bunch are those unbelievers who will not come back to life until the final judgment, where their destiny is defined by the "second death."

Though, again, we are at peace with fellow believers who interpret the Millennial Reign of Christ to be metaphorical, there are valid biblical reasons to view the coming Kingdom as literally on the physical planet. Regarding the duration, God's Word mentions this thousand-year era *six times* in Revelation 20:2–7. Unlike some numbers that have a symbolic meaning—such as "twelve" representing the fullness or completion of God's plans, modeled after the twelve tribes and later twelve apostles—"one thousand" doesn't have quite the same record, and it therefore seems more appropriate to view it in literal terms. One might point out that, in God's timing, a thousand years is like a day and a day is like a thousand years (Psalm 90:4; 2 Peter 3:8). This is why we are not so dogmatic about how long the Millennium (Latin *mille* ["thousand"]; *annum* ["year"]) is going to be when it comes up in conversation with other believers who think it refers to "a really long time." However, if "one thousand years" is tied to a literal reign of Christ on earth, then the principle of consistent application of Scripture would indicate that "thousand" is exactly what it appears to be.

How do we know the reign is a literal one, though, and not a spiritual one?

We believe that's clear based on the fact that the Millennium is *covenantal.* There are a ton of symbols in Revelation, which is why there is a lot of allowance for metaphor in this book, but not all are linked to the New Contract in Christ.

If you look at the Old Covenant, remembering that it was a Contract between God and man, we are reminded that Abraham was promised he would have an uncountable number of descendants (Genesis 12:1–3). When this was fulfilled, it was *not* done through "spiritual children." The covenantal promise of God was given in literal terms and was fulfilled in a literal way, when Abraham's son, Isaac, had Jacob, who was named "Israel" by God, and fathered twelve sons, who bore many sons after that. The same could be true for what Bible readers call the "Palestinian Covenant" regarding the habitation of God's people in the Promised Land of blessing (Deuteronomy 29:1–29; 30:1–10), which they did inherit (again, literally). And when we get to the Davidic Covenant (2 Samuel 7:10–13) that viewed Christ as a King who would rule on David's throne, it would be inconsistent application to suddenly decide that the Contract has shifted toward a metaphor.

With that in mind, we can look a little deeper at what the Millennium describes as a future reality. Recall that in the Prophets section, we listed a number of "Kingdom"-related prophecies that had yet to be fulfilled in Israel's history. Some of those were in reference to the Messiah who will lead that Kingdom, and therefore were fulfilled (as noted) in His First Advent back in the Gospels. (For instance, the Spirit's actions on the Day of Pentecost, prophesied in Joel 2:28 and fulfilled in Acts 2.) Recall the words of the Prophets, Major and Minor, as you read the following, and watch as this still-future event will bring to fruition every last item on their lists regarding the Kingdom of God that have yet to be brought into light. Most definitely, the "rock" that was thrown from out of nowhere and destroyed the many earthly kingdoms in Daniel 2:34, 44 is dominating in this moment of John's vision.

If the bulk of premillennial scholars are correct, then there will be believers and followers of Christ who survive the Tribulation (both Jews and Gentiles), and these folks will not yet be in their glorified bodies like those who were raptured (1 Thessalonians 4:13–18; 1 Corinthians 15:21–23, 51–53), or those who are resurrected in the passages we just read from (Revelation 20:4–6). During the Tribulation, over half the people on earth will perish (6:8; 9:18), leaving a remainder of less than half who, scholars say, will be "regular humans." However, the life span of regular humans will be greatly increased (Isaiah 65:20–22). No wicked men or women will be on the earth during this time, as Christ has defeated them, separating the sheep from the goats (Matthew 25:31–46). (Not all scholars agree with this recap. Some, like Barton, say: "The unbelievers still on the earth after the Battle of Armageddon will have lived through the thousand-year reign of Christ, but as soon as Satan is set free, they will be deceived and ready to *gather…for battle*."[79] This appears to be a minority opinion. Most interpreters we've seen in our research believe that Christ will completely wipe out those who opposed Him at the Battle of Armageddon, and those who oppose Him after the release of Satan are the offspring of Millennium believers.) The scattered remnant of Israel who made it through the Tribulation will be gathered together and converted, and no rebels will be left among them (Ezekiel 20:33–38; Matthew 24:31; Zechariah 12:10–14). This points to the very real possibility that those who have survived and are in their unglorified, physical bodies will still marry and be given in marriage, producing offspring as humans always have. Tribulation survivors of Israel will come to know Christ, having accepted Him as their Savior once and for all when they see Him in His glory (Zechariah 12:10).

Though the saints with glorified bodies will not marry and have children, as they have already crossed over into the system of heaven (which does not follow that of earth; Matthew 22:30), there will be a new generation of offspring born from those who are still in the bodies they were in when they lived through the Tribulation. They will have free will, just as the rest of us, and they must come to know Christ on their own. It is believed that *some* of these children will turn from Him near the end of the Millennium, and it is those who will be called together to war against Christ when Satan is set free for his short, fruitless insurrection against Jesus (Revelation 20:7–10). (It's hard to even imagine this future event when, after all these events in Revelation have come to pass, anyone would still think themselves powerful enough to go against Christ. Not only will Jesus be personally present, but so will the saints, and the faithful men and women from the Old Testament will be there as well, if the scholars are correct in interpreting Daniel 12:2. Nevertheless, the portion of Revelation we're about to get into does seem to teach this very kind of theology. Some academics who have made it their life work to study the Millennial Reign say the following verses describe the Millennium and the uprising that comes at or near its end; according to them, these passages involve the offspring who were born during the Millennium: Isaiah 2:2–4; Zechariah 14:8–21; Ezekiel 34:17–24; Daniel 7:13–14; Micah 4:1–5.)

Christ will be the Ruler over all governments of the world in the way the prophets foretold. That list, scholars say, involves these facts: Jesus' throne will be on Mt. Zion (Psalm 2:6); He will be King (Luke 1:32–33; Matthew 1:1; 21:1–11; Revelation 19:16); He will reign as the Son of David (2 Samuel 7:16; Psalm 89:20–37; Isaiah 11:1–9; Jeremiah 23:5–6; 33:14–26); the saints will reign alongside Him (Isaiah 55:3–4; Jeremiah 30:9; 33:15–17; Ezekiel 34:23–24; 37:24–25; Hosea 3:5; Amos 9:11; 1 Corinthians 6:2; Revelation 20:4–6); His iron-rod rulings will be, uncharacteristically to this earth now, perfectly fair, but swift in the face of opposition (Psalm 2:9; 72:9–11; Isaiah 11:4; Revelation 19:15); He will not favor any person above another, and even the meek and poor will be rulers (Isaiah 11:3–5); animals will not be a danger (Isaiah 11:6–9; 65:25); people will no longer need to teach others about Christ, because all of the world will know Him (Jeremiah 31:34); the economy will be more prosperous, joyful, and peaceful than any kingdom in history (Jeremiah 31:12; Ezekiel 34:25–27; Joel 2:21–27; Amos 9:13–14; Micah 4:2–4; Isaiah 32:17–18; 61:7–10); illness and disease will cease (Isaiah 29:18; 33:24; 35:5–6; 61:1–3; 65:20); there will be obedience to God, as well as an ultimate standard of truth and holiness throughout (Jeremiah 31:33; Isaiah 35:8; 65:16); and, as our favorite part, we will have the full knowledge of God (Isaiah 11:9, Habakkuk 2:14).

Boy! Does this bring unbelievable fulfillment to the Lord's prophecy in Isaiah 9:6–7 or what?! We read there that "the government shall be upon his shoulder." There is no greater way that could be emphasized than in this breakdown! So many of the eschatological prophecies we looked at during our study of the Prophets in the Old Testament are fulfilled in this one-thousand-year reign of Jesus, the Son of David, the Lion of the tribe of Judah (Isaiah 11:1–5; 40:9–10; Jeremiah 23:5–8; Daniel 7:13–14; Malachi 3:1–2).

The Final Defeat of Satan and the Final Judgment (Revelation 20:7-15)

As ABSOLUTELY WONDERFUL and beautiful as the Millennial Reign does sound, believe it or not, it's *still* not the best part. The last couple of chapters of Revelation ramp up to an unfathomable climax!

...But first, there's an old liar who needs to be dealt with, once and for all.

John writes that after one thousand years with Christ on the throne, Satan will be loosed. He will go out and deceive the nations and gather them together for battle. The number of those who participate in the devil's madness are as many as the number of granules of sand by the sea. They will flank the saints and the beloved city, but fire will come down from heaven and devour them. The very same Satan who deceived them will then be thrown into the lake of fire and brimstone, where the Beast and his false prophet will be, and they will all be tormented day and night forever (Revelation 20:7–10).

This is the absolute final time Satan will ever have influence upon the earth. From this day forward, he will remain in the lake of fire with only his evil failures for companions. For us, however, the most awesome, yet possibly frightening, event within humanity is next:

John observes a Great White Throne and the One sitting upon it. Even the earth and sky try to flee from Him, but there is no escaping. All the dead, small and great, now stand in front of God. Even the sea, as well as death and the grave, give up their dead. The books of deeds are opened, along with the Book of Life, and the dead are judged according to their works—what they did, and didn't, do for the Name of God. Death and hell are cast into the lake of fire, which is the second death. Whoever's name was not found written in the Book of Life was cast into the lake of fire (20:11–15).

The nearly unanimous teaching from this group of Scriptures is that the judgment of the "dead" will be for both believers and unbelievers, as supported by 1 Peter 4:5: "Who shall give account to him that is ready to judge the quick [meaning "the living"] and the dead." Another verse that offers helpful (yet chilling) insight related to judgment and the intermediate state between death and resurrection is John 5:25–29:

> Verily, verily, I say unto you, The hour is coming…when the dead shall hear the voice of the Son of God: and they that hear shall live. For as the Father hath life in himself; so hath he given to the Son to have life in himself; And hath given him authority to execute judgment also, because he is the Son of man. Marvel not at this: for the hour is coming, in the which all that are in the graves shall hear his voice, And shall come forth; they that have done good, unto the resurrection of life; and they that have done evil, unto the resurrection of damnation.

By this time in this three-volume work, there may be readers who are curious about this mysterious "intermediate state" where the soul or spirit of a person resides between physical death, the Day of Judgment, and eventual resurrection. There are so many words in the Bible to describe this place ("Sheol," "Hades," "heaven," "hell," "abyss," "bottomless pit," "the deep," "Abraham's bosom," "paradise," and even "tartarus" in some translations) that it's hard to understand God's plans and interactions with this location due to the various treatment the terms are given by various biblical authors. Frequently, the question also arises as to whether we're reading about only one place or several.

One may wonder why we have waited until this moment to discuss this subject...instead of addressing it in, say, the material on Christ's sacrifice on the cross. The reason is simple: Revelation takes the whole of the Bible's teaching on heaven and hell and brings it to a paramount and descriptive climax right about here when the Day of Judgment is in focus.

To shed a little light on this, note that "Sheol" is the Old-Testament form of the New-Testament "Hades" (the two most important and frequently used words in this subject), and generally these are viewed as identical references to the realm where the soul and spirit of the deceased go for a period of awaiting judgment and the resurrection of both the righteous and the wicked (like John states in the quote we just considered).[80] But that is not to suggest the saved and unsaved alike will have the same experience in this seemingly "single" or "one" location represented by numerous terms. Scholars almost unanimously separate this "waiting room" realm into two opposites, or, "two compartments within Sheol-Hades" that are split by a "great gulf" concept.[81] In Luke 16:22–26, we see these segregated domains described as an upper and lower territory—the upper is "Abraham's bosom" or "paradise," while the lower is a terrible place of torment ("abyss," "deep," "bottomless pit," and "tartarus" in the New Testament, also referred to as the "lowest Sheol" in the Old Testament passages of Deuteronomy 32:22 and Psalms 86:13).

From here, scholars also explain that Sheol-Hades is *not* the "final" place for any human soul, wicked or otherwise (a misconception perpetuated by the treatment of terms in certain translations, such as the Authorized Version, which turns the "hell" throughout all of Scripture into an always-eternal Sheol-Hades). For believers, we look forward to the New Heavens, New Earth, and New Jerusalem (discussed in the next section) in our eternity. For unbelievers, the "lowest Sheol" or "Hades" becomes, or at some point "merges with," the lake of fire (which *is* the final place for the wicked). Most scholars see this merger occurring in Revelation 20:14–15, when "death and Hades" are "cast into the lake of fire." If this "merger" theology is correct, then Christ did *not* go "down into hell" between His death and Resurrection (an event captured by the phrase "the harrowing of hell," based on Ephesians 4:9, 1 Peter 4:6, Acts 2:27–31, Romans 10:7, Psalm 16:10, and the Apostles' Creed). Instead, He would have gone "down into Hades" (a far more reliable translation from the Greek), which, at that time, would have been "the temporary abode of the spirits,"[82] making more sense of why the verse in 1 Peter says He preached the Gospel "to them that are dead." (For why would He preach the Gospel to those who are already damned?) It also illuminates how God can be present in this temporary abode up to the point of the merger if it is *not* hell (cf. 1 Samuel 2:6; Job 26:6; Psalm 86:13; 139:8; Isaiah 28:15, 18; Proverbs 15:11; Amos 9:2). Revelation 20:13 explains that the wicked will be brought out of Hades to the Great White Throne Judgment and, like we read in John's vision paragraphs ago, sent back there after they've answered for their deeds (a teaching supported by Psalm 9:17, which states that the wicked will be sent *back to* the lowest Sheol). It is about that point we see that Sheol-Hades and the lake of fire become one for unbelievers.

At the time Christ descended into Hades, a sort of "reorganization" of Sheol-Hades provided a "Good News" message regarding the "release [of] the captives" (Luke 4:18; ASV). This means the righteous dead in that moment were, scholars believe, told through the sermonic announcement of Jesus, personally, that the work that paved their way to an even better fate than "Abraham's bosom" or the "temporary paradise" was completed on the cross just prior. (Most Christians believe—based on a comparison of Ephesians 4:8 and Psalm 68:18 with Proverbs 15:24, Matthew 16:18, and 1 Peter 3:19; 4:6—that the righteous dead were transferred to a heavenly Jerusalem out of the upper Sheol. We have researched this argument from a number of sources and find it to be the most likely. Either way, a Christian who dies today would go to the *current* heaven, which is not Sheol, according to Matthew 16:18 and Revelation 1:18. These verses collectively teach that Jesus, who holds the keys to Hades, defeated it through the cross, and the gates of Hades will never again prevail over the saved. Just as Stephen saw, when we die now, believers go to be with Jesus directly, while He stands at the right hand of the Father, and our spirits are "received" by Him [Acts 7:55, 59].) One day, these souls will join the post-Gospel righteous in the New Heavens/ Earth/Jerusalem, experiencing something completely different than what their Abraham's bosom was at a prior point (discussed by biblical characters in such verses as Genesis 25:8–9; 37:35; Job 14:13; Isaiah 38:10; Psalm 16:10; 49:15; Hosea 13:14; Proverbs 15:24—all of which acknowledge upper Sheol to be a temporary place for the righteous).

All of humanity, regardless of their destiny in "upper" or "lower" Sheol-Hades, will experience consciousness of the soul. This is shown by the fact that Moses, who died and went to "upper" Sheol in the Old Testament, was a participant in the Transfiguration epic of the New Testament (Matthew 17:3). During God's conversation with Moses at the Burning Bush (Exodus 3:1–17), God said He was "the God of Abraham, Isaac, and Jacob." Later, Jesus personally interpreted this to mean that God is "the God of the *living*," despite the fact that these souls had passed into their own afterlife thousands of years prior (Matthew 22:32). So, once we die, whichever place we go, we will be completely aware of either a wonderful, or frightening, constant reality on the other side, like these patriarchs.[83] (See similar language regarding the rich man's experience of consciousness in Luke 16:23–25 and the king of Babylon's in Isaiah 14:9–11, 15–16. All this conversation about a place of torment and punishment makes the idea of the "abyss" opening up and releasing the locust-demons in Revelation 9:1–3 especially terrifying. In fact, this place is so terrible that even the demons pleaded with Jesus not to be sent there in Luke 8:31, because they hoped not to face such horrors before their appointed time, Matthew 8:29 says. And whereas some interpret the realm of the dead to be a literal place at the center of the earth [imagery drawn from colorful Scriptures; see: Matthew 12:40, Jonah 2:2, 6; Ephesians 4:9], we don't feel particularly dogmatic about this theory, as the Bible makes much use of figurative language. Whether it is in or at the earth's core or not, the experience of those who are sent there will be literally felt, as a responsible reading of all Scriptures supports, and as opposed to the contemporary "state-of-mind-misery hell" that a minority of Bible interpreters claim.)

After the souls have reached the end of this "waiting-room" era, we already know the Judgment-Day outcome for those who have ultimately rejected God is not a good one. However, it is fascinating to note that some scholars have questioned whether the Bible truly teaches eternal torment for the unsaved versus a sort of permanent-destruction theory. Some assistance with this idea, as well as visiting the popular question of "how a loving God could send people to hell in the first place," comes from our book *Afterlife*:

> Damnation, according to Scripture, is defined as existence after physical death wherein the soul is separated from the presence of God. But would this be eternal torment (burning in Hell forever) or annihilation (soul and body destroyed in the Lake of Fire and therefore ceasing to exist entirely)? Some scholars assert that the second death, spoken of in Revelation, refers to the concept that once all human souls have reached their final destination, those who are in Hell will be annihilated, citing God's compassion as a motivation for destruction over eternal, irreconcilable torment. God "is longsuffering to us-ward, not willing that any should perish, but that all should come to repentance" (2 Peter 3:9)....

Some contend that…beyond separation from God for eternity, [the second death] is the final termination of the existence of the soul. Reinforcing this concept is that while the Bible speaks of eternal life, the Bible does not use the term "eternal death": "For the wages of sin is death; but the gift of God is eternal life through Jesus Christ our Lord" (Romans 6:23). According to this thought, the suffering in Hell of those who die without Christ is forever terminated when they are cast into the Lake of Fire…. [Further down the line of this theory is the interpretation of the *smoke* rising up from Gehenna (hell) forever, not that the souls of the unsaved are conscious forever.]

Both concepts [eternal torment and annihilation] are terrifying, as each represents permanent and eternal separation from God [and all that is holy and good]….

The English word "hell" is used fifty-four times in the King James Version. Adding the references to Tartarus, Hades, Gehenna, and Sheol, and other terms that translate into the modern English word "hell," we find that there are more than 150 references in the New Testament alone that warn of this place. Furthermore, many of these references were uttered by the Lord Jesus Christ, Himself. There are many who object to the concept of Hell by saying, "A loving God would not send billions of people to a horrible hell; a compassionate God would be more tolerant." However, recall that 2 Peter 3:9 states that God doesn't want people to perish. Jesus paid a high price to offer us the opportunity of salvation, and He makes this precious prospect available to everyone in the world….

[T]he question of why God would send people to Hell if He is indeed a loving and compassionate being is ever-recurring. The answer usually goes like this: "God doesn't *choose* to send people to Hell; they choose it for themselves by rejecting Him." While this may deescalate the general argument, many individuals walk away from such a conversation with lingering questions: questions which, if left unanswered, often call an individual to steer away from a God they feel waives a stick of wrath and judgment.

However, understanding the nature of salvation, why it was necessary, and how it was purchased helps us understand this matter with greater depth, and alleviates frustration left by information gaps that the aforementioned statements do not fill. Some people find the answers to these questions in Scriptures such as Psalm 5:4, which states that no evil can dwell with God, thus, people who haven't accepted Him can't dwell in Heaven with Him, because they have evil that hasn't been [cleansed away] by the blood of Jesus. Others refer to 1 Timothy 2:4, which reminds us [along with the aforementioned 2 Peter 3:9] that God does not want *any* to perish; if this is true, then why wouldn't God force all people to accept His forgiveness—or even forgive them despite their refusal of the gift? If He did this, everyone could go to Heaven, which would be wonderful! Surely a loving God could conduct forgiveness this way if He wanted to, couldn't He?

A vital, yet commonly misunderstood point in all of this is the fact that salvation is a *transaction*: one that Jesus made while on the cross. Anselm, a renowned Christian philosopher of the eleventh century…clarified this convoluted topic for upcoming generations of churches during a time when such doctrine was under debate, by presenting his work on the nature of atonement, *Cur Dos Homo* ("Why God Became a Human Person"). In this thoughtful, pragmatic work, Anselm explained that sin committed by humans is an insult to God's superiority. Because God is the Supreme Being, His standard for justice must be immaculate and unwavering. Anything less than the utmost would likewise be indicative of an inferior being. Thus, the ultimate price must be paid for an insult against the character of the ultimate being. However, because mankind is an inferior being, created *by* God and *for* God, we already owe Him everything that we have, meaning that even in a state of perfection—were it possible to achieve—we would only reach the "expected" status in the eyes of the Most High God. Once sin entered the scene, the lowliness of humanity stooped even farther into the regions of inadequacy. Since our very best would only render us barely acceptable in the first place, adding sin to this dilemma placed us in a deeper state of debt that our very best could never elevate us out of.

The quandary then becomes this: In order for retribution to be made at a standard high enough to appease the justice necessitated by and due to the Most High God, a being of higher rank than a human had to pay the price. In fact, any being inferior to God Himself who attempted to pay such a price would not be able to offer adequate retribution on our behalf, because God's criteria can only accept God-standard levels of payment. However, in order for the transaction to be valid for creatures as lowly as human beings, the penalty had to reach the depraved depths of the realm from which that sin originated: the human, physical realm. For the payment to be *applicable* to humans, it had to descend to the state wherein human sin dwells.

The existence within the physical realm of a perfect God/man Being—Jesus—manifested in a life without sin, and was followed by a sacrificial death, paying the price needed to recreate the pathway between humans and God. In His sacrificial death, Jesus paid the price for our evil deeds. But where does this payment go? Anselm explains that "since God needs nothing, the reward is transferred to sinful humanity; thus God's honor is restored, sin is forgiven, and atonement is achieved."

Many people who ponder a God who "sends people to Hell" often wonder why, if He doesn't want "anyone to perish" (1 Timothy 2:4), He doesn't throw some all-covering "blanket of forgiveness" across all the individuals who would otherwise be condemned to suffer for eternity, inviting them to Heaven (despite their rejection of Him) out of his vast love for all of humanity. The problem with this thinking is this: God has *already* done this very thing—because of His love for humanity—when Jesus (a Being of superior enough rank to pay a price meeting the standard of retribution that God must require) descended to earth and took on human, fleshly form (thus adopting commonality with the lowly, depraved state of humanity, where sin dwells) and then lived a perfect life and gave Himself as a sacrifice, taking on punishment for our sins (thus providing payment and atonement that could reconnect sinful, humankind with the ultimate Most High). Salvation obtained or offered by anything other than a perfect blend of God and man would neither be worthy of offering to God nor applicable to man.

While many might initially view God's forgiveness of man as an emotional connection, the transaction Jesus completed on our behalf was actually technical. Thus, there are rules involved. Because the Most High God had to descend to the lowest low (the human, physical realm) in order to purchase salvation for mankind, humans must likewise choose God while they are in the lowest realm (human) in order to join Him at the highest realm (Heaven)....

Once we leave the corporeal jurisdiction (once we are deceased), it is too late to change our position regarding this transaction, because it must be initiated within the corporeal division, just as Jesus' payment was.

Imagine visiting a store to shop the momentous sales offered on the Black Friday, the day after Thanksgiving. On the way in, you see a store employee handing out coupons saying you can "buy one get one free" of certain popular items. The store's lay-out is structured so that once you are inside, you can't go back out to revisit the woman. In other words, if you don't accept the coupon on the way in, you won't have another chance to get one. Those who turned down the offer will find themselves in line for the purchase, responsible for the full cost of the items with no discount. This is similar to the situation for those who have refused Jesus' offer of atonement. Contrary to what some may claim, the situation isn't that God sends those He loves to Hell, it is that *despite His sacrifice of love*, many choose not to accept His gift. Worse, once we've left the physical realm, we'll never be able to pay for our own atonement, but become permanently ineligible to receive assistance for our salvation. We lock ourselves outside of the transaction by not accepting the "coupon" while we were eligible for it. God will not usurp our will by forcing this salvation on us, because the payment is a gift. This is why, despite the fact that God isn't willing for anyone to perish, *still* some do. He wants us to accept this coverage as a bestowment of His love and generosity while we are living. However, it is no longer a *gift* if it is forced upon us, meaning that unless we accept freely what has been given freely, the forgiveness cannot be attached, negating the gift. Unfortunately, this is why if we deny Him *in this life*, He must deny us *in the next* (Matthew 10:33).[84]

When it comes to judgment, many Christians—both inside and outside academic circles—tend to have a quick and sometimes well-rounded answer for what fate awaits those who do not accept Christ in this life. However, what is *not* unanimously interpreted is how the believers will be judged during this portion of Revelation. Some believe the righteous will be made to face what they did wrong so the mercy of God in forgiveness will be glorified. Most of our sources disagree with this idea, stating that the "judgment" of the "righteous" will be to see how they will be rewarded, not punished or shamed. This is the opinion of: Barton, who says, "Believers will be judged… for rewards"[85]; the writers of *Jamieson, Fausset, & Brown*, who say,

"The godly...shall also be present, not indeed to have their portion assigned as if for the first time (for that shall have been fixed long before, Jn 5:24), but to have it *confirmed* for ever"[86]; Beale, who says the "unbelieving dead" are the focus of judgment, but because "all fall short of the divine standard," the righteous *may* be included in this event, though they will "find refuge" from the fact that their names are in the Book of Life[87]; and many others.

New Jerusalem; New Heavens; New Earth (Revelation 21:1-22)

∞

WHAT IS THE MEANING of life? Everyone has their own answer to this question. However, for the Christian, no matter where the answer *starts*, it *ends* by acknowledging the supreme manifestation of God's will and plan.

Folks, we've reached that climax. The enemy has been forever bound; Antichrist and his pathetic beast-prophet are gone; people have observed the eschatological victories of Christ—*three times* (cross; Revelation judgments; Battle of Armageddon)—and have seen Him reign; the Great White Judgment Day has passed...and we're about to watch as the entire earth melts away and is replaced by a world grander than even that of Eden.

But before we give our own opinions and reflections, we will let the wholly inspired Word of God do the talking:

John watches as a New Heaven and a New Earth appear in a vision. The first heaven and earth are passed away, and the sea is gone. The holy city, Jerusalem, comes down from out of heaven, looking as new and innocent as a bride ready for her husband. A great voice comes from heaven as well, announcing the arrival of the tabernacle of God among men. Now, God, Himself, will dwell with the people. He will be their God, and the people will be His. God will wipe away all the tears from their eyes, and there will be no more death, sadness, crying, or pain, because the things of the old world are passed away. The One on the throne says, "Behold! I make all things new!" Then He says to John: "Write: for these words are true and faithful.... It is done. I am Alpha and Omega, the beginning and the end." The One on the throne goes on to say that He will give the water of life freely to all who are thirsty. These overcomers, He says, will now inherit all things; He will be their God, and they will be His children. But those who were unbelieving—the fearful, the abominable; murderers, adulterers, liars, sorcerers, and witches—have inherited the lake of fire and brimstone, which is the second death (Revelation 21:1–8).

One of the seven angels that had a bowl judgment filled with plague comes up to John and speaks with him, telling him that he will show him the Bride, the Lamb's wife. He carries John away in the Spirit to a great, high mountain, showing John a view of the Holy City, Jerusalem, while it is coming down from heaven. It is filled with the glory of God, and its light is like a precious gemstone, such as Jasper or crystal. There is a giant wall with twelve gates with the names of the twelve tribes of Israel written on them—three gates to the east, three to the north, three to the south, and three to the west—and at the gates are twelve angels. The wall has twelve foundation stones, labeled with the names of the twelve apostles of the Lamb (21:9–14).

The angel that walks with John has a golden measuring stick to measure the city, its gates, and the wall. The city is in the shape of an enormous square, as long as it is wide, and each side is fourteen thousand miles long. By man's measurement, the walls, which are made of jasper, are 216 feet thick. The rest of the city is made of pure gold, which sparkles like glass. The foundations of the city wall are decorated with all manners of precious stones: jasper, sapphire, chalcedony (or agate), emerald, sardonyx (or onyx), sardius (or carnelian), chrysolyte, beryl, topaz, chrysoprasus (or chrysoprase), jacinth, and amethyst. The gates are each carved from a single pearl, and the streets of the city are gold, sparkling like clear glass (21:15–21).

John does not see a temple in the city, because the Lord God Almighty and the Lamb *are* the Temple of the city! No sunshine or moonlight is needed, because the glory of God and the Lamb *are* the light source of the city! The inheritors of salvation amidst all the nations will walk in the light of the New Jerusalem, and the kings upon the earth will walk into the city in glory and honor. The gates will never shut at night, because there is no night, and all the nations will walk into the city in glory and honor. Never again will anything defile Jerusalem—no abomination of any kind, or any deception—because only those whose names are written in the Book of Life will be a part of it (21:22–27).

John is shown a pure river, filled with the water of life, clear as crystal. It flows from out of the throne of God and the Lamb and into the main streets, and on either side of the river, the Tree of Life grows, which bears twelve kinds of fruit. Each month, the fruit is harvested, and the leaves of the tree are keep everyone healthy (22:1–2).

The throne of God and the Lamb will be in this place, and there will be no more curses. God's people will serve Him. They will see His face (finally!), and His name will be in their foreheads. There will never be need for light, like the sun or candles, because the light will always come from God, and the citizens of God will reign alongside Him forever and ever. The angel with John says that this vision of the New Heaven, New Earth, and New Jerusalem is all a true and faithful report, and the God of the prophets sent His angel to show His servants the things that must be done for all of this to transpire (22:3–5).

This is the view of heaven eternal, right here, on earth, in its never-ending and abounding glory. Every sin-stained reality we know today will cease forever.

John's Closing Remarks
(Revelation 22:6-21)

FOR THE REMAINDER of the last chapter, we are brought back to a historical setting for John's closing remarks. The voice is largely in the present-tense, meaning that this is the advice John was giving to the readers of his day:

John switches gears from his reflection on the visions, and writes to the readers, directly, that Jesus will come back soon, and that all those who read the book of Revelation and keep the prophecies therein sacred will be blessed. John then writes that he both saw and heard all of these things. He falls to worship the angel who showed him everything, but the angel refuses to be worshipped, because he is a fellowservant of John's brothers and sisters, the people who keep the book of Revelation holy, so he instructs him to worship only God. Then, the angel says the book of Revelation and all of its prophecies should never be sealed shut. The time is now to share them. Let people continue to make decisions about how they want to live (22:6–11)

John now states the words of Christ: "And, behold, I come quickly; and my reward is with me, to give every man according as his work shall be. I am Alpha and Omega, the beginning and the end, the first and the last" (22:12–13).

To the reader, John writes that those who choose to carry out the Commandments of God are blessed because they will have the rights, and the access, to the Tree of Life, and will be welcome to enter through the gates of the city. People who are like dogs—sorcerers, witches, adulterers, murderers, idolaters, and those who live a lie—will never be welcome to the city (22:14–15).

Again, John states the words of Christ: "I Jesus have sent mine angel to testify unto you these things in the churches. I am the root and the offspring of David, and the bright and morning star" (22:16).

To the readers, John wraps up his statements: The Spirit and the Bride say, "Come." Let him who has ears to hear say, "Come." Let him who is thirsty come, and whoever desires to, let him come and drink of the water of life freely. John testifies personally to anyone who hears the prophecies of this book: If any man (or woman) adds to this book, God will add to him the plagues that are written in it. If any man (or woman) takes away from the words in this book of prophecy, God will take away his name from the Book of Life, and his inheritance in the holy city, and from all the other wonderful things that are written in this book (22:17–19).

John's final words to his readers are these: "He which testifieth these things saith, 'Surely I come quickly.' Amen. Even so, come, Lord Jesus. The grace of our Lord Jesus Christ be with you all. Amen" (22:20–21).

The thing is, the Lord *will* come quickly. By "quickly," Christians have historically grown impatient, comparing every part of God's plan to their own linear concepts of time. But as we have repeatedly discussed, a day is like a thousand years to God, and vice versa. When the Father tells our Bridegroom that the glorious Day of the Lord has come—the hour has arrived when the Bride-sheep will be separated from the Babylon-goats—what will you, personally, be able to say about your own readiness?

This is the end of all things—the end of the revelations of Christ to John concerning the last days, the end of all pain, suffering, disagreement, strife, weakness, illness, destruction, and evil—and the end of the Word of God on the whole matter. For those who reject Christ, this "end" is a terrifying and eternal separation from God. For the rest of us...what does it mean regarding our Christian duty today, in light of the imminency of Jesus' return?

At the very beginning of this work in volume 1, Donna Howell shared a testimony of something she strongly believes that the Spirit told her on the balcony in an Arizona hotel about a Great Spiritual Awakening that is on the very cusp of exploding in our own time. If you recall, what she did *not* share with you, was the other half of that message—the portion that came between the pronouncement of the next Great Awakening and the moment when her request to know what she must do was met with only silence.

Turn the page.

CONCLUSION TO THE WHOLE MATTER[88]

"Is that You, Holy Spirit?" I, Donna Howell, asked several years ago. "Are you telling me You are going to start the next Great Awakening just as Tom Horn, Larry Spargimino, and I predicted a couple of books ago in *Final Fire?*"

"The Great Awakening has already begun," was my answer. "It's in the beginning phases. Only those with eyes to see and ears to hear will see it and hear it. It's starting with My people, My *true* people, while a good portion of the Church and the world around it are asleep and unaware."

This wasn't the first or the last time I would experience something I call a "download." I use that term because, in the two or three total times this kind of epiphany has dawned upon me, the information comes like pop-up windows on a PC—a thousand at once—flooding my mind and soul with information I never could have had time to contemplate or invent.

In the blockbuster-hit film, *The Matrix*, the female lead, Trinity, is on a rooftop in a simulated reality with mayhem all around, and her only escape is via a helicopter she doesn't know how to fly. As her real body and brain are in another building plugged into a computer mechanism, she communicates to her team that she needs a pilot program, and her assistant in the other location uploads the program directly into her consciousness. Her eyelids flutter, and two seconds later, she's an expert pilot. An entire flight curriculum, complete with emergency protocol, has been literally downloaded into her brain and thoughts, opening within her instantly to provide her with the knowledge of a skilled and practiced aviator.

This download, for me, came in a similar fashion. Though I still saw and felt what was literally in front of me—a warm, Arizona breeze and the heat of the midday sun glittering off the glass of commercial city structures and the surface of the hotel pool below—a spiritual flash drive "opened" in my mind.

I saw riots in the news, buildings on fire, folks huddling underground in hiding. I felt the palpable hatred of brother against brother, smelled the sickening stench of human deception, and tasted the bile of the bloodshed of the innocent. Crosses were taken down from churches. Bibles were burning. Pastors were sleeping at the pulpits while their people were screaming. Grandparents were praying in tears and on their knees while their young grandchildren were porn addicts. White powders and needles were scattered around in dumpsters in the alley and nobody cared. Disease and pandemic were spreading like a brushfire and nobody was immune, while women of the night continued to sell themselves for a meal. Busses and other public transportation vehicles were floating slowly downstream in a dirty flood filled with uprooted, dead plants. Military troops fired guns at will. Earthquakes destroyed immense buildings and monuments. Weather maladies of all kinds rained down on vulnerable humanity. Chaos, anarchy, disorder, and confusion were the norm, while hands in high places were shaking on foreign deals from every platform in government.

...And all of this flickered through my head *before* the year 2020 brought even a fraction of this picture to fruition.

My fingers tightened around the railing as I blinked the pictures away. They left as soon as they had come: in an instant. Yet I truly do believe the Lord had said just prior to that moment that a Great Awakening was coming.

What could I possibly do with that contradictory imagery? Which was it? A Great Awakening or a tragic, destitute future for man? What was *actually* coming?

I'd give almost anything to offer up a poetic and picturesque ending—or a dire and *sure* warning like the prophets of old who spoke with the authority of God, Himself, distributing His will to the people in clear-cut terms and instruction—but if you read my testimony at the beginning of this project, you already know what happened next: "What do I need to know?" I asked desperately in my mind. "What's the first move? Tell me what I'm to do and I'll do it!"

There was never a definite answer. In 2020, when I thought for a while that events would escalate to what I had seen and felt, I wondered if I had been given a prophecy that was unfolding in my own time. Then, when things calmed back down, I did what a lot of Christians do: I doubted the whole balcony experience. I never asked for a vision or any such revelation from God, and I wasn't letting my mind wander to terrifying things, telling ghost stories at a campfire, or being spiritual. If you'll remember, at the beginning of the testimony, I was struck mid-thought, while dealing with a publishing company production drama that had escalated that morning. Out of absolutely *nowhere*, I was told that an Awakening was coming while simultaneously receiving an overwhelmingly muddled mountain of startling images.

But surely, I'm human, right? Maybe I caused it after all...? I mean, if there was no answer from the Spirit, then what did all of this amount to?

After my husband and I opened that church in our home (the one I detailed in my testimony opening this book series), and I began to cook for some strong men and women of God while in fellowship and circles of prayer, I was encouraged to hold onto what I had seen and heard. One particular friend of ours gave me great advice, reminding me that sometimes the Lord gives us only partial pictures of His knowledge that He plans to clarify years later. If the balcony experience was nothing, then it wouldn't hurt me to remember it anyway just in case…but if it was *something*, then I better never forget it. Now, though I still don't have all the answers, I feel more certain in my bones that the flash-flood warning has meaning, and that it will continue to reveal aspects of what the Spirit is trying to get across to His people in these times.

I can't help but see how Jesus "appears" in sixty-six books in a row and think that, perhaps, part of the juxtaposition between an Awakening and total societal madness was precise and intentional for such a time as this. Following the terrorist attack of 9/11, religious polls were taken all over the country that showed intense spikes amidst unbelieving populations in belief in God, prayer, and church attendance. Those who had already believed in Jesus before the attacks professed stronger faith and practice than before. A poll from Positive Psychology Online showed that "respondents reported significantly higher levels of spirituality and faith in the two months after 9/11 than respondents who took the survey prior to that date."[89] An astronomically high "90 percent" of Americans reported to rely on "prayer, religion, or spiritual feelings" as a direct result of the attack, and "44 percent" within that number admitted that these "coping mechanisms" were "relied heavily" upon.[90] Another stated that "nine out of ten Americans reported that they coped with their distress by turning to their religion" after 9/11.[91] When COVID-19 hit, similar statistics flooded in. One report states: "Organized religion has been on the decline for decades in the United States. However, during the COVID-19 pandemic, researchers found that online searches for the word 'prayer' soared to their highest level *ever* in over 90 countries."[92] Another poll by the Pew Research Center, in a report titled, "Americans Far More Likely to Say Coronavirus Crisis Has Strengthened Their Faith, Rather Than Weakened It," showed that COVID made 24 percent of Christians' faith in the country stronger, while 47 percent said it didn't affect their faith at all.[93] Yet another report called "Nonbelievers Turn to Prayer in a Crisis, Poll Finds," regarding tragedy in general two years prior to COVID, shows that "among the *non-religious*, personal crisis or tragedy is the most common reason for praying, with one in four saying they pray to gain comfort."[94] Natural disasters are another factor: "Religiosity has increased nine times more in districts across the globe hit by earthquakes compared to those that were spared over the period 1991–2009."[95]

These statistical reports could go on for pages...

I'm not suggesting that the madness-imagery that infiltrated my thoughts is what will *cause* the Great Awakening I believe is in its beginning phases, but I know world events are getting very unstable right now, and Jesus' return is partially reliant upon the actions of His people. And no, I'm not about to tell you that we have to make this wicked world perfect so it will be worthy enough for the Messiah to come back.

In Matthew 24:14 and Mark 13:10, Jesus made it clear that His Second Advent comes only after the Gospel has been preached globally, so the responsibility to evangelize the world and usher in the Messiah's return is ours. The early Church knew this as well, as 2 Peter 3:12 states that they were "looking for and *hasting* unto the coming of the day of God" (emphasis added). Like many verses we've reflected on, the translation here is a little ambiguous. The Greek word for "hasting" is *speudo*, and it means more than just being in a hurry or looking forward to a grand event. In this context, most scholars agree, it refers to cooperating with God "in the redemption of society."[96] In the Lord's Prayer, Jesus made it clear that we should ask for the coming of His Kingdom ("Thy kingdom come"; Matthew 6:10), and in the future, those very prayers are what ushers in the Father's motion to the send the Son back to earth again (Revelation 8:4). Certainly, this doesn't mean it's up to us to "Christianize the world" and aggressively proselytize, shoving mere "religion" down the throats of those who are already on the fence about us "crazy Christian conservatives." Jesus personally warned against that kind of "witnessing" when He said that endeavor only produces a false believer who is "twice the child of hell" as the insincere, apostate Pharisees (Matthew 23:15). Nor does it mean we have to bombard the local voting offices with picket signs and vehemently curse anyone whose social ideas or politics don't please God. Jesus, too, as we discussed throughout the Intertestamental Period and the Gospels, was personally given the opportunity to rise up like a supersoldier against Rome and "Christianize the world" in His day, and He repeatedly refrained from having anything to do with challenging the leaders of the land, even encouraging His followers to respect and pay proper taxes to politicians (Matthew 22:15–22; Mark 12:17). He also explained that no person will ever be able to accurately predict when He returns (Matthew 24:36), so it's not for us to set out with the intention of "kick-starting the Second Coming" through agitating the world that is already less and less tolerant of our beliefs every day.

But the true, life-giving Message of the Gospel will not spread itself. It's clear throughout the New Testament that the Church was built through *people* who were sensitive to the guidance of the Spirit. And God's Word is ripe with proof of a theology called "the delay of God's wrath," meaning that, like the Ninevites of Jonah's time, we can stave off the judgments of Revelation—and the terrifying things I saw on that balcony—by Holy-Spirit anointed evangelism to the lost.

By far, the most popular verse in the Word of God is John 3:16: "For God so loved the world, that he gave his only begotten Son, that whosoever believeth in him should not perish, but have everlasting life." The Gospel never changes, and its directives are solid. Christians are never "off the hook" from having to minister to the "whosoever will."

The New Testament was written two thousand years ago and we are still waiting for Christ's return while watching for the signs. But remember the words of Peter: "But, beloved, be not ignorant of this one thing, that one day is with the Lord as a thousand years, and a thousand years as one day" (2 Peter 3:8). When Paul, the writer of Hebrews, James, Peter, Jude, and John the Revelator spoke of Jesus coming "soon," I'm sure it ignited a feeling within the early Church that the Coming of the Lord would be within their lifetime. Perhaps they looked up every time they walked outdoors, scanning the clouds for any unusual activity. It's probable that some pastors of the fledgling Body used the Epistles from their teaching platforms as they railed passionately about how their listeners should get their things in order and wait prayerfully because Jesus was going to appear in the next few days. Maybe followers said their prayers extra fervently each night, reverent of the notion that it could be their last prayer before something split the heavens apart with a mighty roar during their slumber. And look what happened! These men and women turned the world upside down with the news about Jesus, a "religion" (though I hate to call it that) that would never die!

Following this New-Testament model, the imminency of the Lord's return should not inspire our wish to "kick-start the end"—nor should it cause us to fear the end to the point of evangelizing *just* to delay God's wrath for a while as did the Ninevites. Both of those are human responses to the excitement or fear of the wonderful or scary events in Revelation.

The *true motive* behind the nervous-yet-exciting imminency of Christ's return should be that we are so committed to reaching every last soul we can before they have no time left to make that eternity-altering decision. The focus of our energy in feeling that Christ could literally come back at any second should be in the interest of gathering every soul possible into the circle of saints before any one of them would ever have to make that decision under Antichrist's regime!

Hundreds of thousands of books have been published over the

last two millennia discussing the signs of the coming of the Lord. Many interpreters of Scripture have claimed specific dates or years with confidence, only to face embarrassment when their predictions were incorrect. Others have made prophecy charts showing that most, if not all, of the signs have already been fulfilled, and are warning the world that Christ's return will be this year or the next—especially considering all the headlines regarding Jerusalem's Temple today alongside such heavy, global persecution against Christianity. Though we cannot date-set, and it's best to leave the day and hour to the Lord, with all this waiting, it's easy to understand why some in today's Church have stopped acting as if it could happen any second. One central message of the New Testament is the imminency of Christ's return, and it appears as if many within the Body don't believe Jesus' appearance in the clouds is "imminent" anymore.

It's crucial that we, the Body, are never guilty of being the scoffers mentioned in 2 Peter 3:3–7 who shrug and say the promise of His coming is old news and things are never going to change. We must never allow ourselves to become the scoffers who "deliberately overlook [the] fact that the heavens existed long ago" (ESV), and that we belong to a space and time segregated from the unfathomable workings of heaven that could manifest themselves on earth in a twinkling of an eye (1 Corinthians 15:52). We will never know the day or hour, and we're not supposed to (2 Peter 3:10). But we are commanded: "Therefore, beloved, since you are waiting for these, be *diligent to be found by him* without spot or blemish" (2 Peter 3:14; emphasis added). Note that this verse doesn't say, "Start getting ready pretty soon, guys."

We aren't supposed to just "get" ready, we are to "live" ready, meaning *at all times*.

So what does a reader do after he or she has been shown how Jesus is reflected in every single book of the Word?

If you've read *Final Fire*, then you already know what leads to Great Awakenings. This on-fire scenario has happened before, via revival-hungry men and women throughout history who "lived ready." To them, ministering was about following 2 Peter 3:14 with a diligence to always live in a state of glorious expectation that Christ absolutely can and just might come at any moment (the very definition of "imminent"). There is a reason "living ready" is biblical, because by living ready, we remain on fire, and the lost are irreversibly reached!

I beseech you all. Live as if there really is no guarantee of tomorrow, whether that is on a personal or a global scale. Live as if the next conversation may be the last you ever have with that man or woman. Live as if the next ministerial move you make—the next song you pick for your roster, the next sermon you put on the schedule—is the last one you will ever sing or preach. Live as if the next action you take is in preparation—personally or for others—for the return of Christ. Apply your patience to your internal, unquenchable fire, knowing that "patience" doesn't mean tranquilly staring at a clock; it means carrying out your passion for the Gospel whether you have reason to believe the Second Coming is soon or far away in your own limited concepts of the time/space relationships heaven employs here on earth.

Be accountable to each other for wrongs you commit, treasuring friendship and love above all other acts of holiness. Intercede for each other, not just to put a checkmark on your duty list, but until we see the prayer answered and people healed of physical, emotional, and spiritual malady. Don't say, "I'll pray for you," as casually as the world says, "Let's do lunch sometime." If we "live ready" for the return of Christ, we will observe the very powers of the Almighty God like nothing our planet has ever seen before! Regardless of the unknown date of Christ's Coming: If we truly directed ourselves in a matter that reflected our belief in the imminency of Precious Yeshua—giving ourselves over completely to New-Testament-heroes-style worship and daily conduct—this *current generation* would raise leaders of the Church whose legacies will be documented as changers of the world.

And every generation in the future will be inspired to keep the on-fire, heart-on-the-floor, sold-out, *radical* energy of revival every day, in every minute and every hour, that we exist in this human condition until the sweet Messiah blazes down upon the earth, parting the clouds with a roar!

Things gets serious for the Body when the Body takes things seriously.

Can you hear it?

Can you see it?

Do you feel it?

Do you want it?

Is it pulsating within your blood like it is in mine?

When you close your eyes, do you hear the cheering of uncountable masses who are falling to their knees with weeping and laughter and testimony of the power of God like they did in James McGready's tent revivals of Kentucky in the 1800s? When you close your eyes, do you see the potential future droves and masses of precious people rising out of wheelchairs and jumping across stages like they did in Kathryn Kuhlman's church, or the fifteen thousand teenagers in one single service surrendering their lives to Christ like they did all over the country during the Jesus People Movement of the counterculture era? When you close your eyes, do you, like millions of others talking about it today, "sense" something is in the wind, like an invisible harbinger of conflagration sweeping over the people, preparing to separate the passionate from the apathetic, the sleepers from the leaders, the phonies from the faithful like the Holy Spirit did in D. L. Moody's day?

The Second Advent promises every imaginable and unimaginable relief to our anxious anticipations. Our sins are pardoned. We are forgiven, redeemed. Our names are written in the Lamb's Book of Life. A nod of welcome comes from Peter after death proves to have no sting. Pearly gates open wide to welcome us in to the Holy City that never sleeps and never knows darkness. The throne of God lingers ahead while we walk down a street of pure gold, listening to the deafening praises of the angels about the entrance.

Where there will be no danger.

Where there will be no physical pain.

Where there will be no emotional hurt.

Where there will be no night.

Where there will be no fear.

Where blessing and honor and glory and praise will be lifted to the Giver forever and ever, amen.

The worse things get in the world around us, with quarrels between social groups and kingdoms unable to stand as they fight against themselves, the closer we get to the day Jesus Christ comes to take us all home, and the saints *must* evangelize. If this moment in time and space is the moment in which Christ has positioned you, then believe that God knew you have what it takes to be here, and He has a mission for you. Yes, the world is filled with sinners. Yes, you are one of them. And *yes*, it is the very experiences you've had in your life—including your mistakes and past baggage—that uniquely qualify you as the likeliest soul to reach the lost in your arena of expertise.

The Great Awakening has already begun.

This means you have a job to do.

Go.

Notes

For complete source information on shortened references,
please see the endnotes to volume one.

1. Weber, T. P., "Dispensational and Historic Premillennialism as Popular Millennialist Movements," chapter one in: C. L. Blomberg & S. W. Chung (Eds.), *A Case for Historic Premillennialism: An Alternative to "Left Behind" Eschatology* (Grand Rapids, MI: Baker Academic; 2009), 2.

2. Eusebius of Caesaria, "The Church History of Eusebius," *Ecclesiastical History*, as quoted in: *Eusebius: Church History...* 148.

3. Ibid., 311.

4. Ibid.

5. Ibid., 309.

6. Ibid.

7. Beale, G. K., & Campbell, D. H., *Revelation: A Shorter Commentary* (Grand Rapids, MI; Cambridge, U.K.: William B. Eerdmans Publishing Company; 2015), 2–3.

8. Wilson, M., "Geography of the Island of Patmos (Revelation 1:9)," as quoted in: *Lexham Geographic Commentary...* 621.

9. Carroll, S. T., "Patmos (Place)," as quoted in: D. N. Freedman (Ed.), *The Anchor Yale Bible Dictionary: Volume 5* (New York: Doubleday; 1992), 178–179.

10. Weber, T. P., "Dispensational and Historic Premillennialism..." chapter one in: Blomberg & Chung, *A Case for Historic Premillennialism...* 4.

11. Blomberg, C. L. & S. W. Chung (Eds.), *A Case for Historic Premillennialism: An Alternative to "Left Behind" Eschatology* (Grand Rapids, MI: Baker Academic; 2009), 30.

12. Ibid., 35.

13. Ibid., 40.

14. Ibid., chapter 4.

15. Ibid., 62.

16. Ibid., 63, 76–77.

17. Ibid., 71.

18. Ibid., 74.

19. Ibid., 137.

20. Ibid., 138–142.

21. Mayhue, R., MacArthur, J. F., Jr., Busenitz, N., Waymeyer, M., & Vlach, M, *Christ's Prophetic Plans: A Futuristic Premillennial Primer* (Chicago, IL: Moody Publishers; 2012), 208.

22. Hays, J. D., "Prophecy and Eschatology in Christian Theology," as quoted in: M. J. Boda & G. J. McConville (Eds.), *Dictionary of the Old Testament: Prophets* (Downers Grove, IL; Nottingham, England: IVP Academic; Inter-Varsity Press; 2012), 607.

23. Gentry, K. L., Jr., "A Postmillennial Response to Craig A. Blaising," as quoted in: S. N. Gundry & D. L. Block (Eds.), *Three Views on the Millennium and Beyond* (Grand Rapids, MI: Zondervan; 1999), 228.

24. Ibid., 182–186.

25. Hoyt, Herman A., *The End Times* (BMH Books ed. Chicago, IL: Moody Bible Institute of Chicago; 2012), 91.

26. Souter, A., *A Pocket Lexicon to the Greek New Testament*, on page 197, under "πειρασμός."

27. Ibid., under "πειράζω."

28. Beale, G. K., *The Book of Revelation: A Commentary on the Greek Text* (Grand Rapids, MI; Carlisle, Cumbria: W.B. Eerdmans; Paternoster Press; 1999), 189.

29. Jamieson, Fausset, & Brown, *Commentary Critical and Explanatory on the Whole Bible*, 552.

30. Beale, G. K., *The Book of Revelation...* 217.

31. Irenaeus of Lyons, "Irenaeus *Against Heresies*," as quoted in: A. Roberts, J. Donaldson, & A. C. Coxe (Eds.), *The Apostolic Fathers with Justin Martyr and Irenaeus: Volume 1* (Buffalo, NY: Christian Literature Company; 1885), page 352 in reference to *Heresies* passage 1.26.3.

32. Jamieson, Fausset, & Brown, *Commentary Critical and Explanatory on the Whole Bible*, 555.

33. Morris, L., *Revelation: An Introduction and Commentary: Volume 20* (Downers Grove, IL: InterVarsity Press; 1987), 67.

34. Beale, G. K., *The Book of Revelation...* 242.

35. Morris, L., *Revelation...* 69.

36. Beale, G. K., *The Book of Revelation...* 246.

37. Morris, L., *Revelation...* 70.

38. Beale, G. K., *The Book of Revelation...* 246.

39. Jamieson, Fausset, & Brown, *Commentary Critical and Explanatory on the Whole Bible*, 556.

40. Morris, L., *Revelation...* 73.

41. Ibid., 78.

42. Keith Green, "Asleep in the Light," *The Ministry Years: Volume 1* (Sparrow Records: 1987), track 18.

43. Beale, G. K., *The Book of Revelation...* 289–290.

44. Ibid.

45. Howell, Donna, *Radicals: Why Tomorrow Belongs to Post-Denominational Christians Infused with Supernatural Power* (Crane, MO: Defender Publishing; 2017), 153.

46. Easley, K. H., *Revelation: Volume 12* (Nashville, TN: Broadman & Holman Publishers; 1998), 203.

47. Beale, G. K., *The Book of Revelation...* 376.

48. Ibid.

49. Hoyt, Herman A., *The End Times*, 116.

50. These comparisons are everywhere, but the theories are presented quite succinctly by: Hoyt, Herman A., *The End Times*, 125–126.

51. Beale, G. K., *The Book of Revelation...* 381.

52. Morris, L., *Revelation...* 106.

53. Jamieson, Fausset, & Brown, *Commentary Critical and Explanatory on the Whole Bible*, 568.

54. Morris, L., *Revelation...* 112–113.

55. Ibid., 114; footnote/endnote 6.

56. Bruce, F. F., *Romans...* 218.

57. Hoyt, Herman A., *The End Times*, 142.

58. Bearman, Joshua and Allison Keeley, "The Mad Scramble to Claim the World's Most Coveted Meteorite," December 17, 2018, Wired Magazine, last accessed April 18, 2022, https://www.wired.com/story/scramble-claim-worlds-most-coveted-meteorite/.

59. Ibid.

60. Morris, L., *Revelation...* 124.

61. Beale, G. K., *The Book of Revelation*... 493.

62. Easley, K. H., *Revelation*... 156.

63. Ibid., 157.

64. Barton, B. B., *Revelation* (G. R. Osborne, Ed.; Wheaton, IL: Tyndale House Publishers; 2000), 100.

65. Ibid.

66. We took liberties in explaining most of this on our own based on multiple sources, but much credit goes to the following scholar, who summarized a complicated idea very succinctly: Easley, K. H., *Revelation*, 158.

67. Beale, G. K., *The Book of Revelation*... 506–507.

68. Morris, L., *Revelation*... 133.

69. Barton, B. B., *Revelation*, 111.

70. Morris, L., *Revelation*... 140.

71. Heiser, Michael S., *Angels: What the Bible Really Says About God's Heavenly Host* (Kindle ed.; Bellingham, WA: Lexham Press; 2018), Kindle location 399.

72. Beale, G. K., *The Book of Revelation*... 636–637

73. "Introducing Amazon Go and the World's Most Advanced Shopping Technology," a YouTube video, uploaded on December 5, 2016 by "amazon," last accessed April 20, 2022, https://www.youtube.com/watch?v=NrmMk1Myrxc.

74. Caldera, Camille, "Fact Check: Americans Won't Have Microchips Implanted by End of 2020," August 1, 2020, *USA Today*, last accessed April 20, 2022, https://www.usatoday.com/story/news/factcheck/2020/08/01/fact-check-americans-will-not-receive-microchips-end-2020/5413714002/.

75. McFarling, Usha Lee, "International Team Creates First Chimeric Human-Monkey Embryos," April 15, 2021, *STAT News*, last

accessed April 20, 2022, https://www.statnews.com/2021/04/15/
international-team-creates-first-chimeric-human-monkey-embryos/.

76. "Robot Sophia Got Shut Down by her Creator," a YouTube video, uploaded on January 7, 2018 by "One Click," last accessed April 20, 2022, https://www.youtube.com/watch?v=SNT7qGqmYfc.

77. Horn, Thomas, *The Messenger*... 32–34.

78. This list of theories, and the assigned names, are noted in: Hoyt, Herman A., *The End Times*, 50–55, 65.

79. Barton, B. B., *Revelation*, 243.

80. Hoyt, Herman A., *The End Times*, 36–37.

81. Ibid.

82. Ibid., 40.

83. Ibid., 41–42.

84. Howell, Donna, Josh Peck, and Allie Anderson, *Afterlife: Near Death Experiences, Neuroscience, Quantum Physics, and the Increasing Evidence for Life After Death* (Crane, MO: Defender Publishing; 2019), 265–273.

85. Barton, B. B., *Revelation*, 249.

86. Jamieson, Fausset, & Brown, *Commentary Critical and Explanatory on the Whole Bible*, 600.

87. Beale, G. K., *The Book of Revelation*... 1,034.

88. Some material from this conclusion was taken from: Howell, Donna, *Radicals*, Conclusion.

89. Uecker, Jeremy, "Religious and Spiritual Responses to 9/11: Evidence from the Add Health Study," June 20, 2011, *National Library of Medicine*, last accessed May 15, 2022, https://www.ncbi.nlm.nih.gov/pmc/articles/PMC3118577/.

90. Ibid.

91. Bentzen, Jeanet Sinding, "Natural Disasters Make People More Religious," October 8, 2019, *Oxford University Press Blog*,

last accessed May 15, 2022, https://blog.oup.com/2019/10/natural-disasters-make-people-more-religious/.

92. Morford, Stacy, "Do People Become More Religious in Times of Crisis?" May 5, 2021, *The Conversation*, last accessed May 15, 2022, https://theconversation.com/do-people-become-more-religious-in-times-of-crisis-158849; emphasis added.

93. "Americans Far More Likely to Say Coronavirus Crisis has Strengthened Their Faith, rather than Weakened It," *Pew Research Center*, April 30, 2020, last accessed May 15, 2022, https://www.pewresearch.org/fact-tank/2020/04/30/few-americans-say-their-house-of-worship-is-open-but-a-quarter-say-their-religious-faith-has-grown-amid-pandemic/ft_2020-04-30_covidworship_01/.

94. Sherwood, Harriet, "Non-believers Turn to Prayer in a Crisis, Poll Finds," January 13, 2018, *The Observer*, last accessed May 15, 2022, https://www.theguardian.com/world/2018/jan/14/half-of-non-believers-pray-says-poll; emphasis added.

95. Bentzen, Jeanet Sinding, "Natural Disasters…" https://blog.oup.com/2019/10/natural-disasters-make-people-more-religious/.

96. Green, M., *2 Peter and Jude: An Introduction and Commentary: Volume 18* (Downers Grove, IL: InterVarsity Press; 1987), 164.

9 781948 014632